COARSE FISHING YEAR

COARSE FISHING YEAR

WITH DAVE COSTER, TONY WHIELDON AND ROY WESTWOOD

THE STORM'S OVER AS QUICKLY AS IT BEGAN— BACK TO A BLACK TIP ON THE FLOAT AND I'M INTO A BETTER FISH STRAIGHT AWAY.

HAMLYN

CONTENTS

Published in 1990
by The Hamlyn Publishing Group Limited
a division of The Octopus Publishing Group,
Michelin House, 81 Fulham Road, London SW3 6RB

ISBN 0 600 56959 4

Produced by Mandarin Offset
Printed in Hong Kong

THE APPEARANCE OF THE PERCH IS FOLLOWED BY A STRANGE LULL — I WONDER WHAT'S HAPPENED TO THE CHUB?

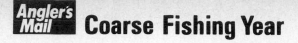

INTRODUCTION

Below: Dave Coster
Right: Tony Whieldon
Below right: Roy Westwood

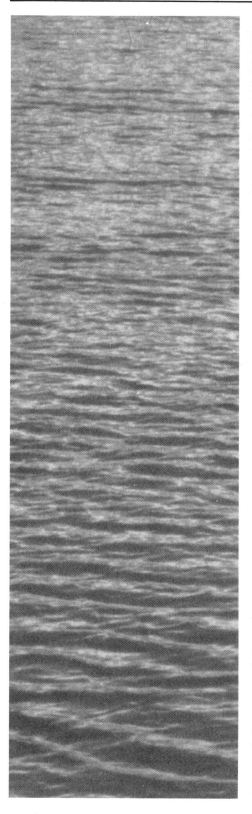

Within weeks of its debut in the centre pages of *Angler's Mail*, we knew the Fishing Diary colour strip was destined to become a classic series that would run and run.

It offered everything the modern coarse angler wanted from pure and basic instruction to advanced techniques – and all graphically presented in a no-nonsense style that is instantly understandable.

Now the most memorable of those diaries recording the weekly adventures of tackle dealer Dave Coster have been collected together in this unique edition embracing the whole fishing year.

I'm aware that many thousands of Fishing Diary addicts are intrigued to know if the storylines are actually true or simply wishful thinking. They also wonder how artist Tony Whieldon manages to accurately paint every blade of grass in favourite swims from Perth to Exeter!

This is the right moment to spill the beans. There is nothing fictional about the Fishing Diary – the ups and downs during Dave's weekly Diary trips are honestly documented at the time. I should know because I shadow him with my cameras when I'm not actually fishing by his side. After every session, Dave writes up the diary with accompanying sketches and these are then expanded on with a series of colour prints capturing the most significant moments of the day.

Dave's swim is photographed from every conceivable angle and it's this comprehensive package of words, pictures and sketches on which Tony Whieldon sets to work in his Devon studio to portray his own evocative interpretation. So now you know – each and every adventure actually happened just as it has been illustrated by Tony Whieldon!

I'm confident you will find this book highly entertaining but I urge you to

study the technical instruction and shrewd tactical thinking that's handed out by Dave along the way. He has got one of the sharpest fishing brains of his generation and continually amazes with his ability to recognise the correct feeding and presentation methods on whichever bank he plants his tackle box.

In fact, Dave has never failed to net a fish and learn a lesson or two in scores of expeditions and that is remarkable considering some of the hostile weather and river conditions we have endured. His flair always saves the day.

On behalf of Dave and Tony, I would like to thank all those fishery owners, specimen hunters and matchmen who have played their part in making the *Angler's Mail* Fishing Diary series a fascinating work of art.

ROY WESTWOOD

Editor, *Angler's Mail*

JANUARY
River Kennet
Newbury, Berkshire

SHALLOWS
SHALLOWS (TROUT)
ISLA
SHALLO
FOOTBRIDGE

SPECIALIST ANGLER BOB JAMES HAS OFFERED ME THE RARE CHANCE TO FISH A PRIVATE TROUT BEAT ON THE BERKSHIRE KENNET. THERE'S BIG ROACH, CHUB, DACE AND GRAYLING — I CAN'T WAIT TO GET STARTED.

BOB JAMES

BOB'S END RIG FOR FISHING BREAD ON THE HOOK WITH A 2/3 MASHED BREAD AND 1/3 MASTERCLASS FEEDBAIT MIX IN THE TINY FEEDER.

PEG LEG STOP

3.5lb ULTIMA

3 ft

18 in

SWAN SHOT

SIZE 8 SEALEY OCTOPUS MATCH HOOK

SMALL CUT DOWN DRENNAN FEEDER

ISOTOPE

NORMAL TIP

QUIVERTIP

ROD

SHIMANO CUSTOM GTM 2500

BOB'S RODS ARE FASCINATING. HE USES FLY FISHING BLANKS SPECIALLY ADAPTED FOR BIG ROACH FISHING. KENT CARPMAN MIKE HARRIS MADE UP THESE RODS AND SPECIAL QUIVER-TIPS. THE VERY SOFT BLANKS PREVENT BIG ROACH FROM ROLLING OFF THE HOOK.

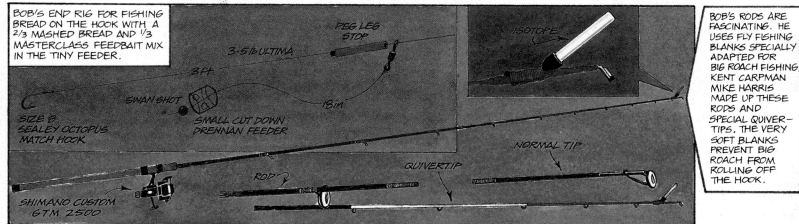

BOB TRIES BOTH SIDES OF THE WEED RACK WITH HIS BREAD BAITS BUT THE CHUB ARE STRANGELY SULLEN. HE WANDERS BACK UPSTREAM TO ANOTHER RACK CONSTRUCTED FROM SCAFFOLDING POLES AND IMMEDIATELY HOOKS INTO A SMALL GRAYLING.

IT SEEMS THE GRAYLING HAVE SHOALED UP IN THE FAST WATER SURGING THROUGH THE RACK WHICH LIES AT THE BACK OF AN ISLAND. *THE ACTION IS FAST AND FURIOUS.*

CARRIER

RAILWAY

AYLING

SHALLOWS
(TROUT, DACE)

EXPOSED
MUD FLAT

SEMI-SHALLOWS
(TROUT, DACE)

DEEPER WATER
(ROACH, CHUB, DACE)

BIG PIKE
LAIR

WEED RACK
AND FOOTBRIDGE

HUT

I'VE STOPPED OFF ABOVE THIS CARRIER WHICH RUNS UNDER THE MAIN KENNET. BOB TELLS ME THE FISH LIE UP JUST BEYOND THE HUMP IN THE RIVERBED CAUSED BY THE CULVERT ROOF.

RAISED BOTTOM FROM MAN-MADE CARRIER UNDER RIVERBED

DEEPER WATER

LOOSE FEEDING SHOULD DRAW THEM UP WITHIN RANGE OF THE STICK FLOAT.

SLACK

MEANWHILE BOB'S SET UP TWO RODS JUST ABOVE THE WEED RACK. HE'S HOPING FOR BIG CHUB WHICH USUALLY RESPOND PRETTY QUICKLY TO BREAD BAITS. THERE'S A MASSIVE PIKE ESTIMATED AT 30lb IN THE SLACK — THAT COULD SPELL TROUBLE.

I'VE BEEN FISHING FOR AN HOUR WITHOUT A BITE WHEN SUDDENLY I PULLED OUT A DACE. NEXT CAST I HOOK SOMETHING BETTER.

A LOVELY 2lb RAINBOW TROUT— LET'S PUT HIM STRAIGHT BACK.

AFTER HOOKING OUT SEVERAL GRAYLING BOB RECOMMENDS I HAVE A GO AS WELL IN THE FAST WATER. WALKING BACK UPSTREAM TOWARDS THE ISLAND I FIND DRAMATIC EVIDENCE OF THE POTENTIAL DROUGHT CRISIS FACING OUR RIVERS. THIS MUDFLAT SHOULD BE COVERED BY WATER AT THIS TIME OF YEAR BUT THE FLOW IS BELOW SUMMER LEVEL. MAKES ME WONDER IF THE ROACH WILL SHOW TODAY.

River Kennet Continued

● Private stretches of water are not necessarily superior to club or day ticket fisheries. This is certainly true on the Kennet where several of the more prolific barbel lengths are accessible on local club cards.

I'M STUCK INTO A SHOAL OF GRAYLING ON A PRIVATE STRETCH OF THE KENNET. THIS IS MY FOURTEENTH IN TWENTY MINUTES.

ALMOST AS THOUGH THEY KNOW THE PIKE HAS HAD ITS FILL THE CHUB START TO MOVE ON BOB'S BREAD FEED AND AS THE LIGHT FADES HE STARTS TO GET A FEW INDICATIONS.

HE WAS JUST GETTING THE BETTER OF THE FISH WHEN A 30lb PIKE DASHED THROUGH THE RACK AND GRABBED IT! BOB FELT HIS LINE GRATING AGAINST THE WOODEN SUPPORTS AS THE PIKE MOVED BACK INTO ITS LAIR. THE ODDS WERE HOPELESS AND BOB TELLS ME IT'S THE SECOND BIG CHUB HE'S LOST TO THE SAME PIKE THIS SEASON.

THE BEST OF THE DAY AT NEARLY 2lb.

NOW THE LIGHT'S FAILING I'M GOING TO SWITCH TO BREAD ON THIS LIGHT BOMB RIG I'VE BEEN EXPERIMENTING WITH RECENTLY.

I CAN SEE WHAT BOB MEANS. THAT WAS THE TINIEST OF MOVEMENTS, ALMOST COULD HAVE BEEN WEED BRUSHING THE LINE BUT IT WASN'T.

IT'S A 12oz DACE.

IT'S GETTING VERY DARK NOW. I WAS REALLY HOPING FOR ONE OF THE KENNET'S BIG ROACH — IF YOU'RE GOING TO GET ONE NOW'S THE TIME.

Salmonhutch Lakes Continued

● There's no Close Season for coarse fishing on Devon stillwaters and many of them remain open all year round. According to fishery owners, this does not appear to affect the well being of the fish or standard of sport.

AFTER MISSING MY FIRST BITE IN THIS SWIM ON THE TOP LAKE AT SALMONHUTCH I'M STRUGGLING AGAIN.

...BUT TONY WHIELDON HAS FOUND

THE FISH GAVE A GOOD ACCOUNT OF ITSELF AND TURNS OUT TO BE THE BEST OF THE DAY AT 7lb — THE SMALL CARP THAT WENT INTO THESE POOLS ARE PUTTING ON WEIGHT FAST.

I DON'T BELIEVE IT — THE HOOK'S PULLED FREE AT THE NET!

TONY'S TAKEN HALF A DOZEN CARP NOW BY STALKING. IT'S NOT REALLY MY STYLE, BUT I THINK I'LL HAVE A GO, AS MY SWIM'S DRIED UP.

FEBRUARY
Perth Harbour
River Tay, Perthshire

I'M OVER 400 MILES AWAY FROM HOME TODAY, FISHING THE RIVER TAY AT PERTH HARBOUR IN SCOTLAND. DAIWA SALES DIRECTOR, JOHN MIDDLETON HAS BROUGHT ME TO THIS BIG ROACH HOTSPOT. I'M GOING TO PUT A PROTOTYPE OF THE NEW DAIWA HARRIER TOURNAMENT ROD THROUGH ITS PACES.

JOHN'S LOOSE FEEDING OVER HIS GROUNDBAIT BUT I'M STARTING A LITTLE MORE CAUTIOUSLY, JUST PUTTING IN REGULAR, SMALLER BALLS OF CASTER-LACED FEED. ALTHOUGH WE'RE 20 MILES FROM THE SEA THERE'S A HUGE RISE AND FALL OF TIDE IN THE HARBOUR AND IT CAN ONLY BE FISHED ON THE EBB. WE'VE HIT IT JUST RIGHT— THE TIDE IS RUNNING OUT UNTIL LATE AFTERNOON.

THAT WAS A BITE! DIDN'T TAKE LONG TO GET A RESPONSE ON DOUBLE MAGGOT. I MISSED THAT ONE BUT I'VE GOT A FEELING THIS IS GOING TO BE A GREAT SESSION. IT'S REALLY MILD FOR MID-WINTER — I'M IN SHIRTSLEEVES.

I DON'T BELIEVE IT. I'VE DROPPED THIS ONE TOO! WHAT ON EARTH'S GOING ON?

THEN JOHN PUTS AN END TO HIS SEQUENCE OF MISSED BITES. HE'S STEPPED UP THE BREAD FEED AND THE ROACH HAVE REALLY GOT THEIR HEADS DOWN.

A NICE 1lb PLUS ROACH.

MY TURN AT LAST AS I FINALLY SUCCEED IN NETTING A GOOD ROACH. THE AVERAGE SIZE OF THE FISH IN THIS HARBOUR LOOKS EXCEPTIONAL.

River Tay Continued

● Roach and pike have always been the traditional targets in lochs and rivers for the small band of Scottish coarse anglers. But clandestine stocking has resulted in a richer mix of species. For instance, there are now shoals of chub and dace in the Clyde and even small pockets of barbel close to Glasgow city centre.

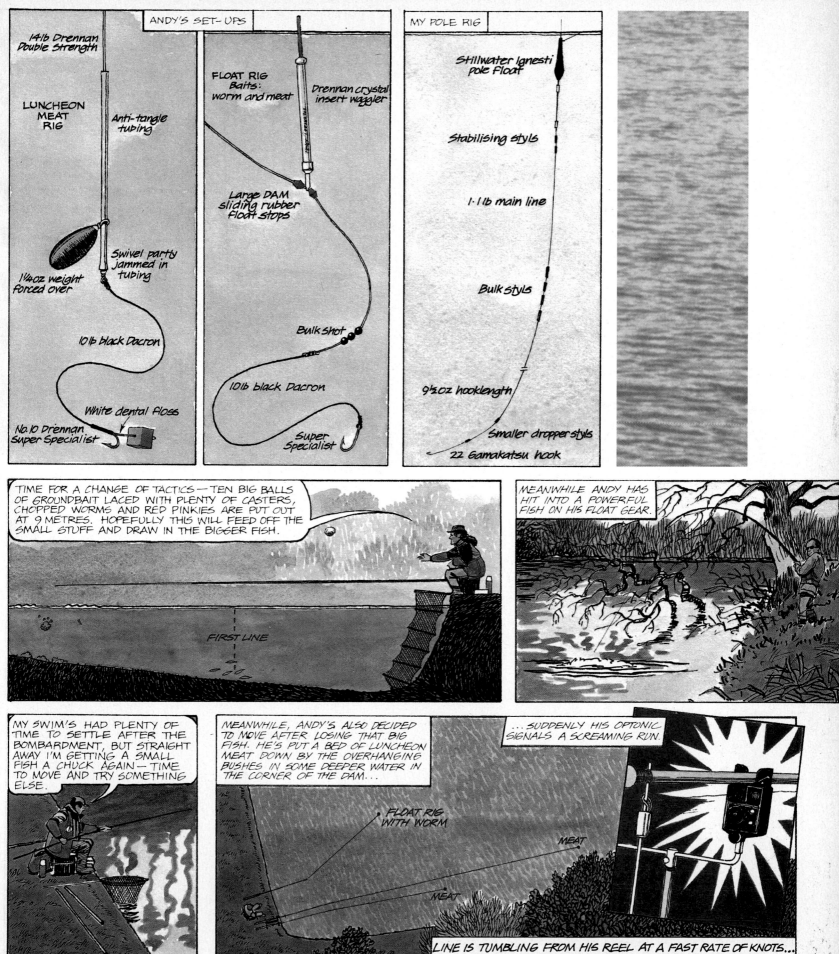

Estate Lake Continued

● Never take anything for granted in coarse fishing. This beautiful, old estate lake might appear to be stuffed with stunted roach and a few middleweight carp but there was at least one pike in the water nearing 20lb and a posse of 3lb perch. Fish populations fluctuate for all sorts of reasons and even a water past its peak is capable of springing a surprise.

ANDY LITTLE HAS STRUCK INTO A BIG FISH AFTER A SCREAMING RUN ON HIS ROD POSITIONED NEAREST THE OVERHANGING BUSHES.

AFTER A SHORT STRUGGLE THE LARGE LANDING NET GOES UNDER THE FISH...

MEANWHILE

I'VE MOVED SWIMS AND FIRST CAST, AFTER CHANGING TO THE WAGGLER, I ALSO HIT INTO SOMETHING A BIT BETTER— A 12oz SKIMMER.

I'M FISHING A 2AAA WAGGLER FIVE ROD LENGTHS OUT AND TAKING FISH STEADILY ON SINGLE WHITE MAGGOT.

ANDY'S SWIM ALSO SEEMS TO HAVE GONE QUIET. ALL HE'S GETTING ARE LINE BITES — ODD, SHORT BLEEPS ON THE OPTONICS.

THE SMALL ROACH ARE BACK IN MY SWIM AGAIN — IT'S A FISH A CHUCK— THEN ANOTHER DEAD SPELL.

CATAPULTING SMALL CLOUDY BALLS OF GROUNDBAIT ONTO THE WAGGLER LINE BRINGS A FEW SMALL BONUS SKIMMERS, BUT BIGGER FISH ARE STILL NOT SHOWING.

THE CARP MAKES A BID FOR THE COVER. ANDY HOLDS IT HARD AND THE FISH SPLASHES ON THE SURFACE, SENDING SHOCK WAVES ACROSS THE LAKE.

...A FIT LOOKING 14½ lb MIRROR.

JUST AS I WAS BUILDING THE SWIM NICELY THE BITES CEASED. I NOTICED THIS A COUPLE OF TIMES IN THE PREVIOUS SWIM — COULD BE A PIKE MOVING IN I SUPPOSE.

ABOUT 100 FISH FOR 6lb. DISAPPOINTING REALLY, CONSIDERING THIS WATER IS NOT NORMALLY FISHED. I'VE A FEELING THESE SMALL ROACH AND SKIMMERS ARE STUNTED...

...THEN AGAIN, ANDY'S TWO CARP LOOKED HEALTHY ENOUGH. THINK I'LL HAVE TO GIVE THIS PLACE ANOTHER GO WITH A DIFFERENT BAIT AND METHOD.

THESE OLD ESTATE LAKES ARE TRULY INTRIGUING WATERS.

FEBRUARY
River Great Ouse
Newport Pagnell, Buckinghamshire

COLIN'S FISHING ABOVE ME ON A NARROWER SECTION AND HAS HIT INTO A BIG FISH STRAIGHT AWAY....

.... ONLY FOR THE HOOK TO PULL FREE AT THE NET. IT WAS A GOOD CHUB.

AT LAST COLIN MANAGES TO DRAW THE FISH TO THE LANDING NET AND REALISES IT'S HIS FIRST EVER BARBEL.

HE'S DELIGHTED! A WELL CONDITIONED FISH OF JUST UNDER 5lb.

AT LAST! A POSITIVE BITE, RIGHT DOWN THE SWIM.

THAT'S BETTER. A 2½lb CHUB.

I TOOK HALF-A-DOZEN SMALL ROACH AND DACE AFTER THAT CHUB BEFORE THE SWIM DRIED UP. I'VE CAST A BOMB RIG BACK INTO THE DEEPER WATER TO SEE IF I CAN DISCOVER WHAT THOSE TINY INDICATIONS WERE BEING CAUSED BY. I'VE ANTICIPATED ONE AND IT'S A REASONABLE FISH.

I'M FISHING THE LINEAR FISHERIES STRETCH OF THE UPPER OUSE IN BUCKINGHAMSHIRE WITH LOCAL BAILIFF COLIN COLBECK WHO WAS THE ORIGINAL CAPTAIN OF THE WELL KNOWN BLACK HORSE MATCHFISHING OUTFIT. HE'S RECOMMENDED THIS SWIM — IT CAN TURN UP BIG CHUB, BREAM AND QUALITY ROACH.

EDDY (BREAM)

ROACH

CHUB

SHALLOWS (CHUB)

I'VE STARTED OFF SEARCHING OUT THE SWIM WITH A WAGGLER RIG. THOSE RUSHES LOOK INVITING, BUT THE DEEPER WATER IN THE FAR BANK EDDY SHOULD HOLD THE BREAM. I'LL SPREAD MY LOOSE FED CASTERS ABOUT UNTIL I GET A BITE.

I'VE ONLY TAKEN ONE GUDGEON ON THE FLOAT. THE WEATHER'S GETTING REALLY NASTY — RAIN AND GALE FORCE WIND. LET'S TRY THE BOMB.

COLIN'S GONE A LONG TIME WITHOUT A BITE SO HE'S SCALED DOWN TO A 1 lb BOTTOM. THIS BRINGS A BOLD BITE ON A SINGLE MAGGOT HOOKBAIT — BUT IT'S CERTAINLY NO CHUB THIS TIME. THE FISH HAS RUN UPSTREAM AND THREATENS TO DISAPPEAR AROUND THE NEXT BEND.

MEANWHILE

I COULD ONLY ATTRACT TINY INDICATIONS ON THE QUIVERTIP. THE DEEPER WATER WON'T RESPOND TO THE WAGGLER SO I'VE BEEN FLICKING A FEW MAGGOTS DOWNSTREAM INTO THE SHALLOWS. LET'S RUN A FLOAT DOWN THERE.

DAMN! THE HOOK PULLED FREE — FELT LIKE A GOOD ROACH TOO.

A BIT DISAPPOINTING, JUST THE ONE CHUB AND A SMATTERING OF BITS. THE RIVER WAS SOCK-ON A WEEK AGO BUT THE COLOUR'S DROPPED OUT AND THE WIND AND RAIN MADE TACKLE PRESENTATION VERY DIFFICULT. WONDER WHERE THOSE BREAM ARE HIDING?

MARCH
Twyford Farm
Warwickshire Avon

DESPITE HIS OBVIOUS DISAPPOINTMENT AT BEING PIPPED AT THE POST FOR THE MATCHMAN OF THE YEAR TITLE, PAUL NEWELL IS FISHING BRILLIANTLY. HE'S WON 3 MIDWEEK OPENS IN THE SPACE OF SIX DAYS. TODAY HE STARTS THE MATCH ON A STICK FLOAT RIG...

TODAY I'M FISHING A MATCH ON THE WARWICKSHIRE AVON AT TWYFORD WITH NEW SHAKESPEARE MATCHMAN OF THE YEAR DAVE HARRELL AND RUNNER-UP PAUL NEWELL. DAVE'S NOT DRAWN BADLY ON WILMOTS (PEG 2) AND PAUL'S GOT A GOOD 'UN TOO, PEG 10 AT WILMOTS — OPPOSITE THE MOUTH OF A BROOK. I'VE BEEN DRAWING REALLY BADLY LATELY. YES, I'VE DONE IT AGAIN ! PEG 105, A REAL NO-HOPER THEY TELL ME.

DAVE HARRELL IS FISHING A SIMILAR TWO-PRONGED APPROACH BUT IS USING A 14 METRE POLE FOR THE NEARSIDE LINE.

MY SWIM IS A RIGHT 'BIRDCAGE' HIGH BANK BEHIND AND SURROUNDED BY TREES AND BUSHES. THE WAGGLER IS OUT, WITH SLACK ACROSS AND THE MAIN FLOW 1/3RD OF THE WAY OUT. I'LL START ON 9 METRES OF POLE, BUT THE INSIDE FLOW IS VERY ERRATIC.

NOTHING ON THE POLE AS YET, SO LET'S TRY THE MAGGOT FEEDER ACROSS. I'M NOT THAT CONFIDENT — THE ONLY FAR-BANK FEATURE IS ANOTHER FISHING STAGE.

IT'S A CLOSE BATTLE WITH DAVE HARRELL WHO'S ALSO CATCHING A FEW ON THE POLE.

Warwickshire Avon Continued

● Matches along the Avon are among the most competitive in the country. On popular stretches like Twyford Farm, matchmen know the precise potential of each and every swim and the best methods to adopt. There is really no need for coarse fish surveys on waters like this – the matchmen soon know if there has been the slightest shift in fish numbers!

MATCHMAN OF THE YEAR DAVE HARRELL HAS TAKEN A FEW BITS ON HIS POLE. NOW HE'S MOVING HIS ATTACK ACROSS THE RIVER, HOPING FOR CHUB ON THE WAGGLER...

MY MATCH ON THE WARWICKSHIRE AVON AT TWYFORD IS GOING BADLY. I'VE ONLY TAKEN A RUFFE AND A GUDGEON FROM AN UNFANCIED PEG. THE FAR SIDE FEEDER LINE IS ALIVE WITH MINNOWS AND THE INSIDE FLOW IS ALL OVER THE PLACE.

ARCH RIVAL PAUL NEWELL IS ALSO ON THE WAGGLER, HE'S LANDING A 1lb CHUB.

WHILE THERE'S ANOTHER DING-DONG BATTLE GOING ON BETWEEN DAVE AND PAUL, I'M STILL SEARCHING FOR A TAKING METHOD. I SPOTTED A BLEAK TOPPING SO I'VE QUICKLY SET UP A SURFACE RIG ON A SIX METRE POLE.

I'LL PUT IN SOME SLOPPY GROUNDBAIT EVERY CAST WITH A FEW FREE PINKIE OFFERINGS.

SLIM POLE FLOAT

SMALL BULK (Nº 9s)

10oz

22 BARBLESS

THIS IS BETTER. I'VE TAKEN 16 OF THESE HUGE BLEAK IN 16 CHUCKS

WITH JUST AN HOUR TO GO I'VE GOT ABOUT 3lb OF GUDGEON AND BLEAK, NOT ENOUGH I FEEL FOR A SECTION WIN. I NOTICED A BIG FISH ROLL OVER BY THE FAR BANK STAGING — COULD HAVE BEEN A PIKE ....

...BUT I'LL TRY A BIGGER HOOK AND SOME LUNCHEON MEAT ON A STRAIGHT BOMB RIG JUST IN CASE IT WAS A CHUB OR BARBEL.

MARCH
River Lea
Cheshunt, Hertfordshire

I'M FISHING 10½ METRES OUT, PRESENTING MY RIG JUST UP THE LEDGE ON THE FAR SIDE. I'VE TRIED PUTTING IN NEAT JOKERS BUT WITHOUT RESPONSE. NOW I'LL TRY SIX BALLS OF JOKER LACED GROUNDBAIT. A BIT EXTREME, BUT THE DISTURBANCE OFTEN BRINGS IN SOME FISH, AND SURPRISINGLY QUICKLY.

MY MATCHFISHING MATES TOLD ME OF SOME FINE ROACH AND BLEAK WEIGHTS ON THE LEA NAVIGATION AT CHESHUNT AND I'VE DECIDED TO INVESTIGATE WITH THE LONG POLE AND BLOODWORM. TO MY RIGHT IS BRITISH GROUNDBAITS ANGLER STEVE LINNEY — HE'S GOING FOR THE BLEAK.

I COULDN'T GET A BITE IN THE FIRST SWIM SO I'VE MOVED UP NEAR THE LOCK. STEVE'S STRUGGLING TOO AND HAS ALSO SWITCHED SWIMS TO FISH OPPOSITE A BOAT TURNING BAY. HE RECKONS THE WATER'S A LOT CLEARER THAN WHEN IT PRODUCED THE GOOD WEIGHTS IN A MATCH THREE DAYS AGO.

AH, A BITE AT LAST!

A TINY PERCH.

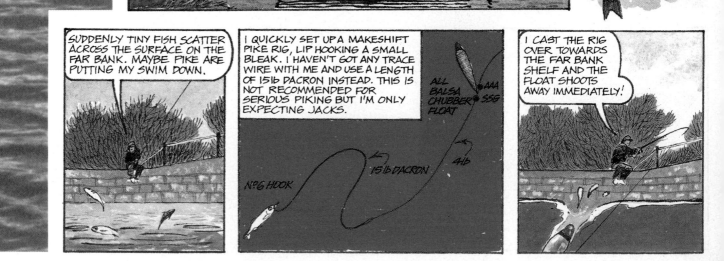

SUDDENLY TINY FISH SCATTER ACROSS THE SURFACE ON THE FAR BANK. MAYBE PIKE ARE PUTTING MY SWIM DOWN.

I QUICKLY SET UP A MAKESHIFT PIKE RIG, LIP HOOKING A SMALL BLEAK. I HAVEN'T GOT ANY TRACE WIRE WITH ME AND USE A LENGTH OF 15lb DACRON INSTEAD. THIS IS NOT RECOMMENDED FOR SERIOUS PIKING BUT I'M ONLY EXPECTING JACKS.

ALL BALSA CHUBBER FLOAT
AAA
SSG
15lb DACRON
4lb
No.6 HOOK

I CAST THE RIG OVER TOWARDS THE FAR BANK SHELF AND THE FLOAT SHOOTS AWAY IMMEDIATELY!

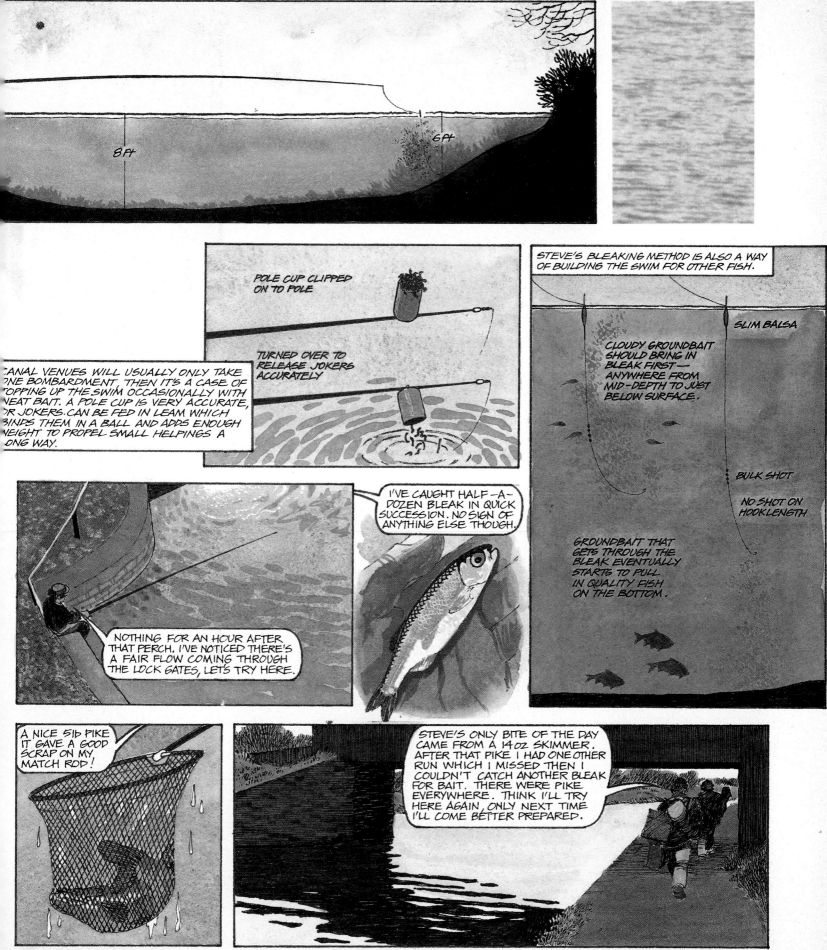

POLE CUP CLIPPED ON TO POLE

TURNED OVER TO RELEASE JOKERS ACCURATELY

CANAL VENUES WILL USUALLY ONLY TAKE ONE BOMBARDMENT. THEN IT'S A CASE OF TOPPING UP THE SWIM OCCASIONALLY WITH NEAT BAIT. A POLE CUP IS VERY ACCURATE, OR JOKERS. CAN BE FED IN LEAM WHICH BINDS THEM IN A BALL AND ADDS ENOUGH WEIGHT TO PROPEL SMALL HELPINGS A LONG WAY.

STEVE'S BLEAKING METHOD IS ALSO A WAY OF BUILDING THE SWIM FOR OTHER FISH.

SLIM BALSA

CLOUDY GROUNDBAIT SHOULD BRING IN BLEAK FIRST— ANYWHERE FROM MID-DEPTH TO JUST BELOW SURFACE.

BULK SHOT

NO SHOT ON HOOKLENGTH

GROUNDBAIT THAT GETS THROUGH THE BLEAK EVENTUALLY STARTS TO PULL IN QUALITY FISH ON THE BOTTOM.

I'VE CAUGHT HALF-A-DOZEN BLEAK IN QUICK SUCCESSION. NO SIGN OF ANYTHING ELSE THOUGH.

NOTHING FOR AN HOUR AFTER THAT PERCH. I'VE NOTICED THERE'S A FAIR FLOW COMING THROUGH THE LOCK GATES, LET'S TRY HERE.

A NICE 5lb PIKE IT GAVE A GOOD SCRAP ON MY MATCH ROD!

STEVE'S ONLY BITE OF THE DAY CAME FROM A 14oz SKIMMER. AFTER THAT PIKE I HAD ONE OTHER RUN WHICH I MISSED THEN I COULDN'T CATCH ANOTHER BLEAK FOR BAIT. THERE WERE PIKE EVERYWHERE. THINK I'LL TRY HERE AGAIN, ONLY NEXT TIME I'LL COME BETTER PREPARED.

8 FT

6 FT

River Lea Continued

● Like the majority of our rivers, the Lea is unrecognisable from the meandering, overgrown waterway of Izaak Walton's day. Bends and bankside cover have been obliterated. Heavy industry and ugly housing estates crowd its banks. But somehow the resilient coarse fish stocks survive the pressures of the 20th century and provide a means of escapism for millions . . .

> I'VE BROUGHT DEADBAITS AND SPINNERS WITH ME TODAY TO HAVE A GO FOR THE PIKE WHICH WERE VERY ACTIVE LAST WEEK. LET'S JUST SEE IF THE BLEAK ARE STILL AROUND FIRST.

> THERE SEEMS TO BE A HUGE SHOAL TUCKED RIGHT IN THE MOUTH OF THE LOCK. I'M GETTING THEM QUITE FAST.

SLIM BALSA BLEAKER
4ft
BULK No.10s
9oz
22 BARBLESS

> NOTHING. THE IRONY IS THAT THE WATER'S A LOT MORE COLOURED THIS WEEK AND I HAVEN'T GOT BLOODWORM AND JOKER WITH ME. I BET IF I HAD I'D HAVE A NETFULL OF ROACH.

> LET'S TRY A DEADBAIT ON THE FAR SHELF.

Tony Whieldon

DEADBAIT RIG
SSG
SSG
SINGLE HOOK WIRE TRACE
LIP HOOKED DEADBAIT

> I'M USING A STYL RIG AND PICKING THE FISH UP BY TRIPPING A SINGLE PINKIE ALONG THE BOTTOM.

THIN BALSA FLOAT WITH WIRE STEM

BULK STYLS

SMALL STYL DROPPERS

> THAT'S AMAZING – A BITE STRAIGHT AWAY FROM A 4oz ROACH . . . .

> . . . . AND ANOTHER.

● PIKE ACTIVITY AREA LAST WEEK.

THESE FRENCH BLEAK FLOATS REALLY ARE VERY GOOD. THEY'RE PAINTED A LIGHT GREY SO YOU CAN SPOT THEM TILTING OVER IF A BLEAK RUNS WITH THE BAIT.

BLEAK

WELL, THE BLEAK MUST BE SHOALED UP TIGHT IN THE LOCK MOUTH FOR A REASON. LET'S TRY THE SURROUNDING WATER WITH A PLUG.

THE DEADBAIT DOESN'T SEEM TO BE PULLING ANY ATTENTION. I THINK I'LL TRY THE LONG POLE. I'LL PUT HALF-A-DOZEN BALLS OF PINKIE LACED GROUNDBAIT IN AT 10 METRES.

THE FISH ARE A LOT MORE ACTIVE THAN LAST WEEK. BY FEEDING CLOUDY GROUNDBAIT AND A FEW PINKIES I'M GETTING PLENTY OF BITES.

HOW IRONIC, LAST WEEK I HAD THE BAIT TO DO THIS AND GOT PESTERED BY PIKE, TODAY I ONLY HAD HALF A PINT OF PINKIES AND I'VE CAUGHT LOADS OF ROACH AND PERCH.

APRIL
River Shannon
Eire

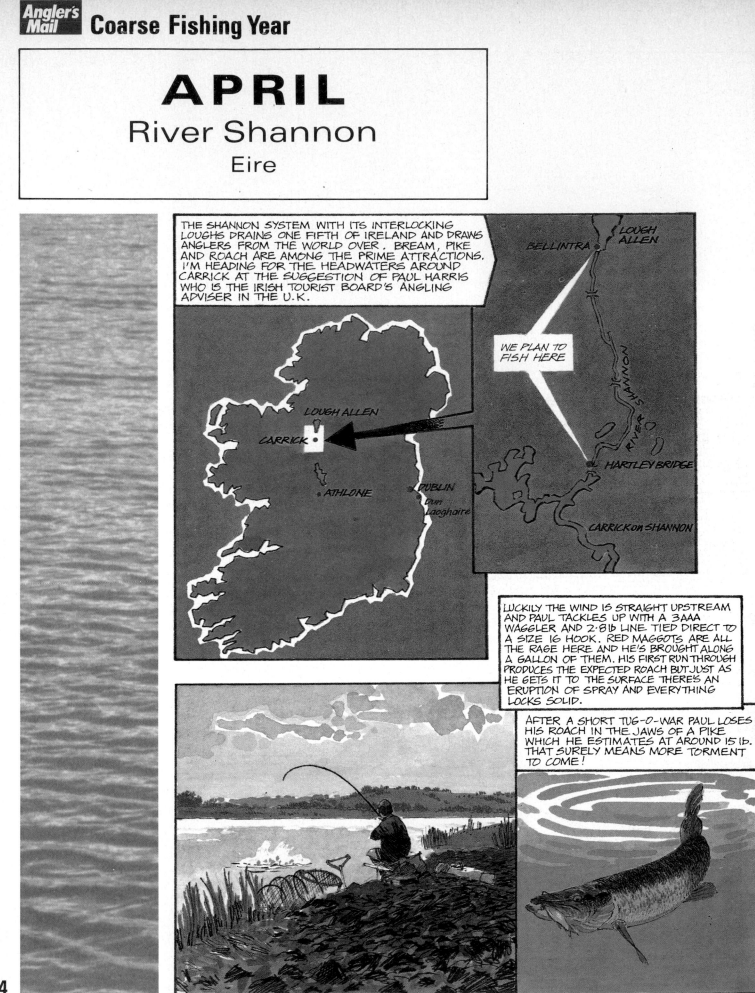

THE SHANNON SYSTEM WITH ITS INTERLOCKING LOUGHS DRAINS ONE FIFTH OF IRELAND AND DRAWS ANGLERS FROM THE WORLD OVER. BREAM, PIKE AND ROACH ARE AMONG THE PRIME ATTRACTIONS. I'M HEADING FOR THE HEADWATERS AROUND CARRICK AT THE SUGGESTION OF PAUL HARRIS WHO IS THE IRISH TOURIST BOARD'S ANGLING ADVISER IN THE U.K.

WE PLAN TO FISH HERE

LOUGH ALLEN

BELLINTRA

LOUGH ALLEN

CARRICK

ATHLONE

DUBLIN
Dun Laoghaire

RIVER SHANNON

HARTLEY BRIDGE

CARRICK on SHANNON

LUCKILY THE WIND IS STRAIGHT UPSTREAM AND PAUL TACKLES UP WITH A 3AAA WAGGLER AND 2·8lb LINE TIED DIRECT TO A SIZE 16 HOOK. RED MAGGOTS ARE ALL THE RAGE HERE AND HE'S BROUGHT ALONG A GALLON OF THEM. HIS FIRST RUN THROUGH PRODUCES THE EXPECTED ROACH BUT JUST AS HE GETS IT TO THE SURFACE THERE'S AN ERUPTION OF SPRAY AND EVERYTHING LOCKS SOLID.

AFTER A SHORT TUG-O-WAR PAUL LOSES HIS ROACH IN THE JAWS OF A PIKE WHICH HE ESTIMATES AT AROUND 15 lb. THAT SURELY MEANS MORE TORMENT TO COME!

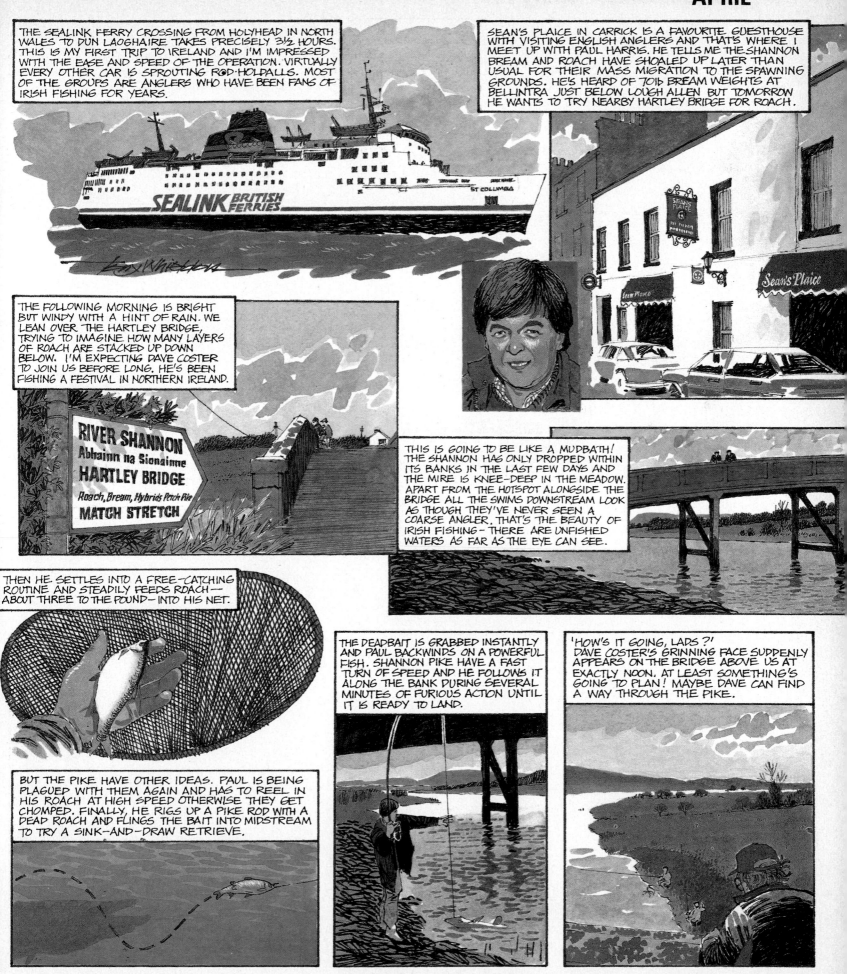

THE SEALINK FERRY CROSSING FROM HOLYHEAD IN NORTH WALES TO DUN LAOGHAIRE TAKES PRECISELY 3½ HOURS. THIS IS MY FIRST TRIP TO IRELAND AND I'M IMPRESSED WITH THE EASE AND SPEED OF THE OPERATION. VIRTUALLY EVERY OTHER CAR IS SPROUTING ROD-HOLDALLS. MOST OF THE GROUPS ARE ANGLERS WHO HAVE BEEN FANS OF IRISH FISHING FOR YEARS.

SEAN'S PLAICE IN CARRICK IS A FAVOURITE GUESTHOUSE WITH VISITING ENGLISH ANGLERS AND THAT'S WHERE I MEET UP WITH PAUL HARRIS. HE TELLS ME THE SHANNON BREAM AND ROACH HAVE SHOALED UP LATER THAN USUAL FOR THEIR MASS MIGRATION TO THE SPAWNING GROUNDS. HE'S HEARD OF 70lb BREAM WEIGHTS AT BELLINTRA JUST BELOW LOUGH ALLEN BUT TOMORROW HE WANTS TO TRY NEARBY HARTLEY BRIDGE FOR ROACH.

THE FOLLOWING MORNING IS BRIGHT BUT WINDY WITH A HINT OF RAIN. WE LEAN OVER THE HARTLEY BRIDGE, TRYING TO IMAGINE HOW MANY LAYERS OF ROACH ARE STACKED UP DOWN BELOW. I'M EXPECTING DAVE COSTER TO JOIN US BEFORE LONG. HE'S BEEN FISHING A FESTIVAL IN NORTHERN IRELAND.

RIVER SHANNON
Abhainn na Sionainne
HARTLEY BRIDGE
Roach, Bream, Hybrids Perch Pike
MATCH STRETCH

THIS IS GOING TO BE LIKE A MUDBATH! THE SHANNON HAS ONLY DROPPED WITHIN ITS BANKS IN THE LAST FEW DAYS AND THE MIRE IS KNEE-DEEP IN THE MEADOW. APART FROM THE HOTSPOT ALONGSIDE THE BRIDGE ALL THE SWIMS DOWNSTREAM LOOK AS THOUGH THEY'VE NEVER SEEN A COARSE ANGLER. THAT'S THE BEAUTY OF IRISH FISHING - THERE ARE UNFISHED WATERS AS FAR AS THE EYE CAN SEE.

THEN HE SETTLES INTO A FREE-CATCHING ROUTINE AND STEADILY FEEDS ROACH — ABOUT THREE TO THE POUND— INTO HIS NET.

THE DEADBAIT IS GRABBED INSTANTLY AND PAUL BACKWINDS ON A POWERFUL FISH. SHANNON PIKE HAVE A FAST TURN OF SPEED AND HE FOLLOWS IT ALONG THE BANK DURING SEVERAL MINUTES OF FURIOUS ACTION UNTIL IT IS READY TO LAND.

'HOW'S IT GOING, LADS?' DAVE COSTER'S GRINNING FACE SUDDENLY APPEARS ON THE BRIDGE ABOVE US AT EXACTLY NOON. AT LEAST SOMETHING'S GOING TO PLAN! MAYBE DAVE CAN FIND A WAY THROUGH THE PIKE.

BUT THE PIKE HAVE OTHER IDEAS. PAUL IS BEING PLAGUED WITH THEM AGAIN AND HAS TO REEL IN HIS ROACH AT HIGH SPEED OTHERWISE THEY GET CHOMPED. FINALLY, HE RIGS UP A PIKE ROD WITH A DEAD ROACH AND FLINGS THE BAIT INTO MIDSTREAM TO TRY A SINK-AND-DRAW RETRIEVE.

River Shannon Continued

● Dave Coster joins Westwood at Hartley Bridge to take up the story

THE FLOW HERE IS A LITTLE PACEY AND I'VE PUT MORE SHOT DOWN THE RIG THAN USUAL FOR THIS TYPE OF WAGGLER SET-UP. THE WATER'S VERY CLEAR SO I'M GOING TO FISH A 1lb HOOKLENGTH — LIGHT FOR IRELAND, BUT I'M MAINLY EXPECTING ROACH.

I'VE REALLY BEEN LOOKING FORWARD TO THIS OUTING ON THE SHANNON. LAST TIME I FISHED THE RIVER TWO YEARS AGO I MISSED OUT ON BREAKING THE 100 lb BARRIER ON A MATCH BY JUST ONE FISH. I HAVEN'T GOT LONG TODAY SO ROY WESTWOOD HAS PACKED UP AND PAUL HARRIS IS GOING TO SLOW DOWN ON HIS FEEDING TO GIVE ME A CHANCE TO GET AMONG THE ROACH WHICH ARE SHOALING DOWNSTREAM OF HARTLEY BRIDGE.

DIDN'T TAKE LONG FOR A BITE. NOT A BIG FISH THIS, BUT THE SIGNS ARE THERE THAT THE SWIM'S COMING TO LIFE.

THE WEATHER'S VERY CHANGEABLE THIS AFTERNOON — I HAVE TO KEEP SWITCHING FLOAT TIPS FROM BLACK TO ORANGE SO I CAN SEE WHAT'S GOING ON

I CAN SEE BLACK BETTER WHEN THE SUN'S OUT...

AND HAVE TO CHANGE TO ORANGE WHEN IT'S OVERCAST.

WE'VE ALREADY HAD RAIN SQUALLS — NOW IT'S PELTING DOWN HAIL THE SIZE OF MARBLES.

A PRIME 14-OZ. ROACH.

FOR A MINUTE I THOUGHT I'D CONNECTED WITH A BIG BREAM, BUT IT'S SUDDENLY STEAMED OFF DOWNSTREAM — I RECKON A BIG PIKE'S GRABBED A ROACH.

NEARLY GOT THE PIKE INTO MY NET THERE! HE JUST LET GO OF THE POOR ROACH AT THE LAST MINUTE.

River Shannon Continued

● The exodus of English anglers to Eire every Close Season is a ritual sustained by unrivalled catches of bream, roach and tench. Thousands cross the sea to fill their nets and recharge their batteries of enthusiasm. Ireland offers stacks more fish than back home and has realised many a dream.

I'VE BEEN EXPERIENCING A BIT OF PIKE TROUBLE AT HARTLEY BRIDGE ON THE SHANNON. I'VE STOPPED USING GROUNDBAIT AND GONE FURTHER OUT ON THE WAGGLER. WHEN I CATCH A ROACH I'M BULLYING IT IN OVER THE NEARSIDE LEDGE – WHERE I SUSPECT THE PIKE ARE LYING UP.

BY JUST LOOSE FEEDING I'VE PULLED THE ROACH UP IN THE WATER. I'VE HAD TO MOVE MY BULK SHOT UP TO COMPENSATE AND THE BITES ARE COMING THICK AND FAST NOW.

PAUL HARRIS OF THE TOURIST BOARD RECKONED THE ROACH WERE RUNNING ON THE QUALITY SIDE HERE YESTERDAY, BUT TODAY THERE ARE LOTS OF SMALL FISH, WHICH IS SLOWING ME DOWN A BIT.

IF THEY WERE ALL THIS SIZE I'D BE ON THE WAY TO A MASSIVE WEIGHT – AS IT IS THOUGH I STILL THINK I'M GOING TO PUT A PRETTY BIG CATCH ON THE SCALES.

HERE WE GO AGAIN! I WAS A FRACTION SLOW WITH THIS ROACH AND A BIG PIKE'S GRABBED IT!

I PLAYED THE PIKE FOR FIVE MINUTES AND HE LET GO LIKE THE LAST ONE SO I'VE GOT MY ROACH BACK.

I'VE MOVED UPSTREAM INTO THE WHITE WATER SWIMS JUST BELOW LOUGH ALLEN. I'VE HEARD BREAM HAVE BEEN MOVING HERE. THE FLOW'S VERY POWERFUL SO IT'S A ROD-IN-THE-AIR JOB TO KEEP THE FEEDER STILL.

A GOOD DROPBACK BITE AND I'M INTO A FISH! THIS FEELS LIKE A BREAM HAS TAKEN MY WORM AND MAGGOT COCKTAIL.

THE FISH FOUGHT WELL IN THE FAST CURRENT AND FELT MUCH BIGGER THAN IT IS – A 1lb SKIMMER.

Tri-Lakes Fishery Continued

● The chain of mature gravel pits to the west of London produce more giant fish than many anglers realise. Numerous 40lb carp have gone unreported because of strict rules of secrecy imposed by the controlling clubs. There are almost certainly British record tench and bream on the loose within 45 minutes of Hyde Park Corner.

REGULAR LOOSE FEEDING IS BRINGING THE FISH UP, BUT AFTER THAT GOOD SPELL THE BITES ARE GETTING HARD TO CONNECT WITH AGAIN.

I'VE STARTED TO CATCH TENCH WELL OFF THE BOTTOM ON MY WAGGLER RIG. THE FISH ARE REALLY FEEDING WELL NOW — A 2½lb TENCH FOLLOWED BY A 1lb CRUCIAN, THEN A 1½ TENCH AND ANOTHER CRUCIAN.

I WONDERED WHAT ON EARTH THAT WAS AT FIRST! ONE OF THE CARP ANGLERS IS USING A RADIO CONTROLLED, MODEL BOAT TO DROP BOILIES BY A BUSH ON THAT ISLAND. THAT'S THE MOST ACCURATE LOOSE FEEDING I'VE EVER SEEN.

I'VE TRIED SWITCHING TO A FEEDER, BUT THE FISH WOULDN'T HAVE IT IN THE SHALLOW WATER. THE BOMB SEEMS BEST — TOPPING THE SWIM UP WITH A COUPLE OF BALLS OF GROUNDBAIT OCCASIONALLY...

...THAT WAS A FINICKY BITE BUT I HIT IT!

NEXT CAST

ANOTHER FISH — THIS ONE TOOK ON THE DROP.

IN THREE HOURS FISHING THIS IS THE ONLY ACTION I'VE HAD. I MOVED INTO SHALLOWER WATER AND PUT A WAGGLER OUT AND AFTER A COUPLE OF FINICKY TOUCHES HOOKED AN EEL OF ABOUT A POUND.

LET'S PUT IT BACK. THE OTHERS HAVEN'T CAUGHT, SO WE'RE GOING TO MAKE A QUICK DASH OVER TO ANGLERS' PARADISE AT BEAWORTHY.

ZYG GREGOREK HAS BUILT SEVERAL INTERESTING LAKES HERE. HE'S MADE ANGLERS PARADISE INTO A SUCCESSFUL VENTURE WHERE ANGLERS CAN ENJOY FIRST CLASS ACCOMMODATION AND INTERESTING, VARIED FISHING.

THE LAKE COMPLEX

BEGINNERS CARP LAKE

TENCH LAKE

E.T. LAKE

MAIN CARP LAKE

PIXIE LAKE

FLOAT FISHING LAKE

FISH FARM

SPECIMEN LAKE

KOI LAKE

GROUNDBAIT

THERE'S 3FT OF WATER JUST OFF THE ISLAND SO I'VE BAITED UP WITH GROUND-BAIT AND HEMP — I'M LOOSE FEEDING MAGGOTS OVER THE TOP.

LONG INSERT WAGGLER

AAA

BB

Nº 10

Nº 10

THE SPECIES IN HERE ARE BLUE ORFE AND GOLDEN TENCH. I'M USING A LONG INSERT WAGGLER AND HAVE SET THE TACKLE SLIGHTLY OVERDEPTH SO THE LAST Nº 10 RESTS ON THE BOTTOM. THIS DELICATE SET-UP WILL SHOW LIFT BITES AS WELL AS CONVENTIONAL ONES.

I'VE TAKEN HALF A DOZEN SMALL ORFE — NOW I'VE GOT A REALLY POWERFUL FISH ON.

WHAT A BEAUTY! A BLUE ORFE OF A POUND OR SO — THINGS ARE GETTING INTERESTING!

Anglers' Paradise Continued

● Zyg Gregorek could not speak a word of English when he arrived here as a Polish refugee. From that unlikely beginning he has built up a booming angling holiday centre in the wilds of Devon with top quality fish stocks bred and reared in his own stewponds.

MAY
Broadland's Fishery
Hampshire

M27 Motorway
N
Boat Bay
M-Way Bank
Blackwater Corner

EDITOR, ROY WESTWOOD AND I HAVE BEEN INVITED TO FISH BROADLANDS LAKE, ALONGSIDE THE M27 MOTORWAY IN HAMPSHIRE. FISHERY MANAGER MARK SIMMONDS HAS STOCKED HEAVILY WITH BIG FISH OVER THE PAST DECADE AND WE COULD CATCH ANYTHING FROM OUR SWIM BEHIND THE ISLAND — MAYBE EVEN A RECORD CRUCIAN.

I'M STARTING ON A BIG BODIED WAGGLER, LOCKED BY NEARLY 4 SSGs.

MEANWHILE

ROY'S CATAPULTED KING PRAWN BOILIES UNDERNEATH AN OVERHANGING BRANCH AND ALSO UP AGAINST THE EXPOSED ROOTS OF A TREE WHICH HAS FALLEN ON THE ISLAND, LEAVING A DEPRESSION IN THE MARGINS. THERE'S AN AIR OF EXCITEMENT TODAY BECAUSE A 35lb MIRROR CARP WENT INTO THE WATER RECENTLY.

AS FOR ME, I'LL BE HAPPY TO CONNECT WITH THE PROLIFIC BREAM AND ROACH SHOALS — THIS FEELS LIKE A SKIMMER ALREADY!

MY STEADY FEEDING IS BRINGING PLENTY OF BITES NOW, FIRST FROM SKIMMERS AND QUALITY ROACH . . . .

BY NOW I'M WELL INTO DOUBLE FIGURES ON THE FLOAT, BUT THE WIND PICKS UP AND THIS METHOD DIES.

TIME TO TRY THE FEEDER.

Loop to loop
Large loop
Bead
Link swivel
Cage Feeder

A GOOD BITE STRAIGHT AWAY! — THIS FEELS A MUCH BETTER FISH!

SURE ENOUGH, A BRIGHT EYED TENCH OF 3lb SCRAPS ALL THE WAY TO THE NET.

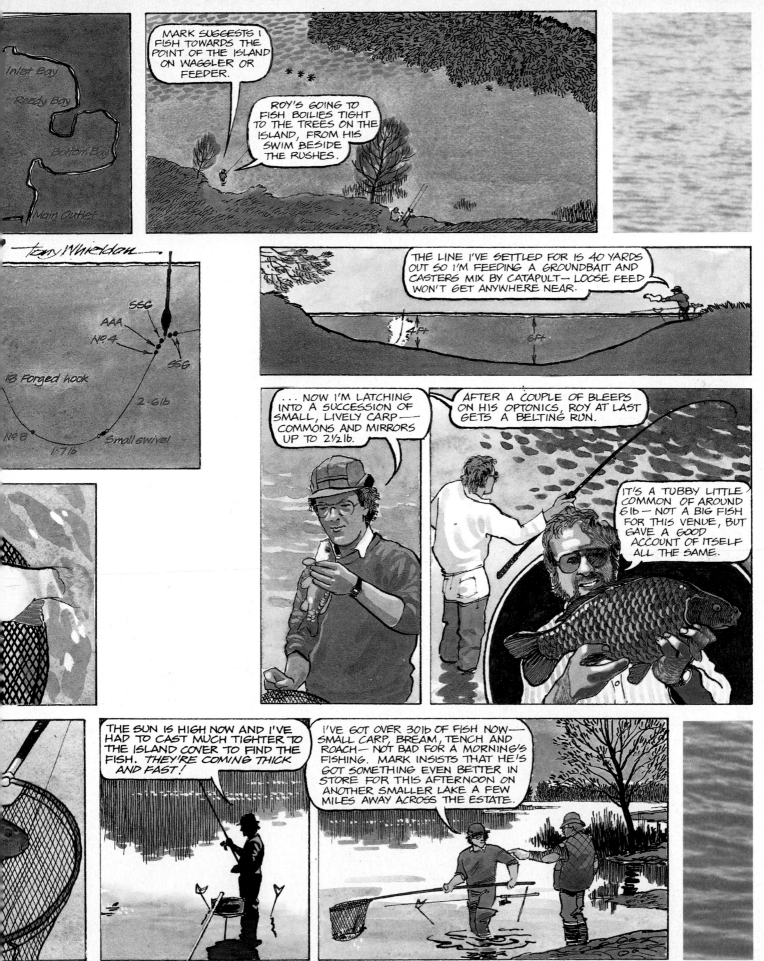

Broadlands Fishery Continued

● It's possible to get a glimpse of the carp action at Broadlands from the fast lane of the M27 – and that is probably one of the reasons for its success. But good communications are only part of the story. Shrewd management and stocking have kept the day ticket rods rolling in. It all helps compensate for the decline of the salmon on the Test – thank goodness for carp runs!

I HAVEN'T GOT A GREAT DEAL OF TIME SO I'M GOING TO CONCENTRATE ON THE POLE, ON THE NARROW SIDE OF THE ISLAND. THERE'S PLENTY OF FISH TOPPING AGAINST THE ISLAND, SO I'LL TRY TO ENTICE THEM OUT RATHER THAN DUMP MY TACKLE ON TACKLE ON THEIR HEADS.

AFTER SPENDING THE MORNING ON THE MAIN LAKE AT BROADLANDS, I'VE DRIVEN TO ANOTHER PART OF THE ESTATE TO TRY THE NEW LONGBRIDGE FISHERY. THERE'S ABOUT 25 SWIMS, NOT A BIG WATER, BUT I'M ASSURED BY FISHERY MANAGER MARK SIMMONDS IT'S SOLID WITH FISH.

THE SWIM IS BUBBLING WITH FISH. THE MORE FEED I PUT IN, THE FASTER MY HOOK-BAIT IS SNAPPED UP! THIS IS A MORE NORMAL LAKE FISH, A 1lb SKIMMER.

FISHING SLIGHTLY OVERDEPTH, I'M STARTING TO MISS A LOT OF BITES. I THINK THEY'RE FALSE INDICATIONS CAUSED BY FISH KNOCKING INTO MY LINE.

I'VE HOOKED ONE AND IT'S A 1lb GOLDEN ORFE, THE FIRST TIME I'VE CAUGHT ONE OF THESE BEAUTIFUL FISH.

TEN MINUTES LATER AND I'VE TAKEN EIGHT GOLDEN ORFE BETWEEN 12oz AND 1lb .... NOW THEY'VE MOVED OFF.

THAT'S DIFFERENT A RAINBOW TROUT, TAILWALKING MY ELASTIC TO FULL STRETCH.

Met Police Pit Continued

● The bottoms of gravel pits are often heavy on tackle. Line soon weakens when scuffed over bars and it's as well to run the last few feet between your fingers periodically to feel for abrasions. If there's a rough spot then take the trouble to retackle. Remember to store the discarded line carefully in your tackle box for safe disposal at home.

I'VE BEEN PLAYING THIS GOOD FISH FOR SEVERAL MINUTES ON LAKE TWO, PART OF THE PRIVATE MET. POLICE FISHERY AT WEST DRAYTON.

AFTER THAT CRUCIAN IT'S BACK TO MISSED BITES. TIME FOR A CHANGE TO THE LONG POLE.

THIS IS MY BIG TENCH POLE RIG. LATELY I'VE ONLY BEEN USING 2¼lb ELASTIC IN THE POLE INSTEAD OF THE WIDELY USED 4lb. I FIND THIS STRETCHES MORE. THE FISH HERE ARE SO BIG THAT YOU CAN GET BREAK-OFFS ON 1.7lb WITH THE THICKER GEAR.

FIBRE STEM BODIED POLE FLOAT WITH THICKISH TIP.

2.6lb

Nº4s

1.7lb

Nº11

Nº11

THAT'S INTERESTING. THERE'S A DEFINITE DEPRESSION IN THE BOTTOM ON 10½ METRES. I'LL CONCENTRATE ON THIS. I'M FISHING 10 METRES OR SO SHORTER THAN THE WAGGLER LINE.

I'VE PUT A COUPLE OF HELPINGS OF EXPO IN AND TOPPED UP WITH HEMP AND CASTER— ALREADY THE SWIM IS ERUPTING WITH BUBBLES.

THE FLOAT SUDDENLY SHOT AWAY! THIS IS A REALLY EXCITING WAY OF CATCHING TENCH! AND EFFECTIVE! I WOULDN'T HAVE CONNECTED WITH THAT BITE ON THE WAGGLER IN THIS AWKWARD SWIM.

THE SECRET WITH THE POLE AND LIGHT TACKLE IS TO GET THE FISH ON THE SURFACE BEFORE YOU START UNSHIPPING SECTIONS. OTHERWISE YOU END UP WITH 15 FOOT OF POLE AND 15 FOOT OF ELASTIC PLUS YOUR END TACKLE STRETCHING OUT OF CONTROL.

AN EVEN BIGGER TENCH!

WHAT'S THIS?! ROY WESTWOOD SAYS HE'S BEEN TO THE CARS TO FIND SOMEONE'S SMASHED HIS WINDOW AND TRIED TO RIP OUT THE RADIO!

THE POLICE HAVE BEEN CALLED. WHAT A PITY WE'LL HAVE TO CALL IT A DAY PREMATURELY, JUST WHEN IT WAS TURNING INTO A BRILLIANT SESSION. THESE FOUR FISH WEIGHED 20lb, THE BEST TENCH WAS 6½lb.

River Trent Continued

● It is said that the most accomplished stick float anglers in the land did their apprenticeship on the Trent. But the days of roach duels and delicate float skills were rudely shattered when chub and barbel became more dominant. Then the swimfeeder increasingly entered the fray and changed the tempo of Trent matchfishing for all time.

HE LOSES THE PIKE AFTER A HECTIC BATTLE AND REELS IN A SEVERELY MANGLED ROACH.

TRENT STICK FLOAT MAESTRO PETE WARREN HAS HAD AN 8oz ROACH GRABBED BY A BIG PIKE AT THE TAIL END OF HIS SWIM.

PETE'S HOOKED ANOTHER PIKE AND THIS TIME LANDS A FOUR POUNDER ON HIS FINE TACKLE.

I'VE MIXED UP SOME HEAVY GROUNDBAIT TO SEE IF I CAN GET THE FISH DOWN AND SORT OUT SOME BETTER ONES.

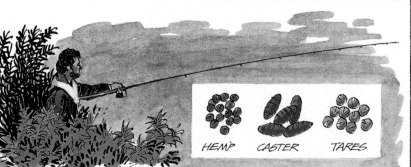

THE EMERGING PATTERN SEEMS TO BE THAT THE TRENT IS TURNING BACK TO THE HEMP AND CASTER APPROACH, AFTER A COUPLE OF YEARS DOMINATED BY THE MAGGOT.

PETE ALSO FINDS TARES PULL THE ODD BETTER ROACH, BUT THEY ARE NOT WORKING CONSISTENTLY TODAY.

BUT ON THE POLE LINE THE NUMEROUS SKIMMERS AND SMALL ROACH WILL ACCEPT ANYTHING! I'M PROVING THIS BY CATCHING ON A WHOLE SPECTRUM OF BAITS OVER THE GROUNDBAIT.

HEMP   CASTER   TARES

MEANWHILE I'M STARTING TO CATCH SMALL ROACH AND SKIMMERS ON 9 METRES OF POLE.....

...USING A 1 GRAM BODIED POLE FLOAT WITH AN OLIVETTE RIG AND STYL WEIGHTS ON A 12oz HOOKLENGTH. MY SWIM IS SLOWER AND DEEPER THAN PETE'S.

SMALL STYL WEIGHTS

OLIVETTE

I'VE BEEN USING LOOSE HEMP AND CASTER FEED WITH MAGGOTS ON THE HOOK, BUT IN THIS DEPTH I'M GETTING PESTERED WITH SMALL FISH. A CASTER ON THE HOOK GETS SHELLED EVERY TIME.

THIS SEEMS TO SETTLE THE SWIM AND HE'S BACK ON THE ROACH.

BUT THE WEED PROBLEM IS STARTING TO AFFECT HIM TOO, AND HE LOSES AN ESTIMATED 2lb+ ROACH ON THE THICK NEARSIDE WEED AFTER IT MAKES A LAST DITCH PLUNGE FOR FREEDOM.

IT'S INTERESTING THAT PETE'S SO CONFIDENT IN HIS SHOTTING PATTERN HE ONLY THINKS IT NECESSARY TO MOVE HIS FLOAT POSITION TO KEEP IN CONTACT WITH THE FISH.

THERE'S NOT A GREAT DEAL IN IT BY THE TIME WE CALL IT A DAY. PETE'S PIKE HAS TIPPED THE BALANCE IN HIS FAVOUR, BUT HE'S IMPRESSED BY THE SMALL FISH CATCH I'VE PUT TOGETHER ...

..FROM THE DEEPER WATER WHERE THE TOP CURRENT MAKES HIS STICKFLOAT METHOD IMPOSSIBLE. IF HE DRAWS THIS AREA ON THE NEXT MATCH HE'S GOING TO FISH THE POLE.

JULY
Linear Fisheries
Newport Pagnell, Buckinghamshire

WELL, I'VE GOT A FEELING I'M GOING TO HAVE A PASTING TODAY. I'M FISHING WITH ROY WESTWOOD AND FISHERY MANAGER LEN GURD ON POPLAR LAKE, PART OF THE LINEAR FISHERIES COMPLEX AT NEWPORT PAGNELL.

ROY'S OPTONICS ARE SOUNDING VERY REGULARLY — THERE CERTAINLY ARE A LOT OF FISH OUT THERE. I THINK HIS GARDNER ROD POD SYSTEM IS BRILLIANT. HE CAN MOVE OPTONICS, RODS, THE LOT IN SECONDS IF HE WANTS TO REPOSITION HIS GEAR.

THERE HE GOES AGAIN!

THERE'S A CANADA GOOSE NESTING JUST BEHIND THE BUSH ON THE ISLAND AND ROY'S GOT A SWAN NESTING OPPOSITE HIM. NEITHER BIRD HAS SHOWN ANY CONCERN — THE SWAN ACTUALLY CAME OVER TO US, LOOKING FOR TIT-BITS.

Linear Fisheries Continued

● Fishery manager Len Gurd is an accomplished carp angler with a record of heavyweights second to none. But his skills as an artist and book illustrator are probably now more widely known. A great deal of the inspiration for his fish drawings arises from his daily observations at Linear as he walks the banks checking all is well – both with anglers and fish.

JULY
River Thames
Cookham, Berkshire

I'VE HAD A BIT OF A BARNEY WITH OUR CAPTAIN. HE'S CERTAIN THE MAGGOT FEEDER AND LONG POLE WILL DO MOST DAMAGE, BUT I RECKON THE OPEN-END FEEDER IS MILES BETTER ON THIS PART OF THE THAMES.

RAY BENTON

ESSEX COUNTY HAVE DRAWN COOKHAM IN THE D.F.D.S. CHALLENGE ON THEIR STRETCH OF THE MIDDLE THAMES AND WITH THE REST OF THE SQUAD I'M OUT PRACTISING FOR THE BIG DAY. NONE OF US REALLY KNOW WHAT TO EXPECT, BECAUSE THE COOKHAM STRETCH HAS BEEN PRIVATE FOR YEARS.

THE DROP-BACK OCCURS BECAUSE THE FEEDER IS JUST HOLDING BOTTOM AND ANY INTERFERENCE WITH THE HOOKBAIT DISLODGES IT.

2. FEEDER MOVES

3. CURRENT BOWS LINE BUT TENSION IS RELEASED

4. TIP FALLS BACK

1. FISH PULLS ON HOOKLENGTH

I THOUGHT THAT WAS AN EEL. YOU CAN TELL BY THE WAY THEY SUDDENLY STOP DEAD AND THUMP THE ROD TIP LIKE MAD.

THE BOATS HAVE STARTED TO MOVE AND BITES FADE. MAYBE THEY'VE PUSHED THE FISH FURTHER OVER — THERE'S 20 YARDS OF WATER TOWARDS THE FAR BANK, RELATIVELY UNDISTURBED. TO MY RIGHT, ANDY'S STRUGGLING ON THE MAGGOT FEEDER.

THERE'S ONLY ONE THING TO DO NOW AND THAT'S PUT OUT 6 MORE BALLS OF CASTER PACKED GROUNDBAIT INTO THE LESS DISTURBED AREA...

MAIN

River Thames Continued

● There is free fishing on the Thames below Staines Stone and it's a fact that the biggest fish in the river are swimming in the bloodworm rich tidal reaches. Barbel of nearly 20lb and carp to more than 30lb are known to be present. Access is impossible to some of the most promising marks, particularly around Battersea.

MY THAMES PRACTISE SESSION WITH ESSEX COUNTY AT COOKHAM HAS BEEN RUDELY INTERRUPTED BY A BOAT. IT CUTS ACROSS MY LINE AND I LOSE THE END TACKLE.

A LULL IN THE BOAT TRAFFIC GIVES ME TIME TO EXPLORE THE QUIETER WATER FURTHER OVER. A SWITCH TO WORM AND CASTER ON THE HOOK AND I'M STARTING TO FIND 3 TO 4lb BREAM, EVEN TAKING THEM ON THE DROP.

IT'S INTERESTING THAT I'VE CAUGHT ONLY BREAM AFTER STARTING ON THE OPEN-END FEEDER, WHILE SOME OF MY TEAM-MATES HAVE PICKED UP THE ODD CHUB AFTER SWITCHING FROM MAGGOT. THE CHUB HAVE GONE FOR THE CASTER AND WORM BUT WERE COUGHING UP MAGGOTS. STRANGE!

I THINK I'D BETTER CALL IT A DAY. I'M BEGINNING TO AMASS A REALLY BIG WEIGHT— I'M NEARLY 30lb AHEAD OF EVERYONE ELSE! I WANT TO LEAVE SOME FISH FOR MATCH DAY IN CASE WE DRAW THIS PEG.

WE'VE DECIDED IT'S GOING TO BE THE OPEN-END FEEDER FISHED WELL ACROSS THE RIVER AS OUR MAIN LINE OF ATTACK AND TO FEED THE POLE LINE AS A RESERVE SHOULD THE FEEDER NOT WORK FOR EVERYONE. WE CAN'T BELIEVE HOW WELL THE RIVER IS FISHING— IS THERE A TRICK WE'VE MISSED?

POSTSCRIPT ON MATCH DAY ITSELF COOKHAM AND OURSELVES MAKE AN EARLY START TO MISS THE WORST OF THE BOAT TRAFFIC. PETE CLAPPERTON HAS CHOICE OF ODDS OR EVENS AS AWAY SIDE CAPTAIN AND PICKS EVEN PEGS. HIS CHOICE HAS SWUNG AGAINST ODDS, BECAUSE BIG WEIGHT PEG IS NUMBER 4 ON THE DAY.

THE MATCH TURNS INTO A BIT OF A STRUGGLE, AGAINST ALL EXPECTATIONS. TRAFFIC IS VERY BUSY AND TO ADD TO THE COMPETITORS PROBLEMS THERE'S A YACHT RACE ON THE VENUE TOO.

I DON'T MIND SHARING WATERS WITH OTHER INTERESTS, BUT SOME HOLIDAY BOATERS ARE GIVEN 2 MINUTES INSTRUCTION AND THEN LET LOOSE TO DO THEIR WORST. PITY THEY'RE NOT TAUGHT SOME WATER CRAFT.

AFTER ADDING SIX GOOD BREAM I'VE MADE MY POINT! CAPTAIN PETE CLAPPERTON HAS ORDERED HIS TROOPS TO SWITCH TACTICS WITH AMAZING RESULTS. APPARENTLY ALL THE SWIMS HAVE COME TO LIFE.

THAT BOATER KINDLY SLOWED DOWN WHEN HE SAW ME PLAYING A GOOD FISH. THANKS MATE!

THIS IS REALLY TURNING INTO A MARVELLOUS SESSION. THE MORE FEED I INTRODUCE, THE MORE FISH MOVE INTO THE SWIM. BIG SLABS SOME OF THEM TOO.

GORDON BLANKS HAS TAKEN OVER A HUNDRED FISH, MOSTLY DACE, ON THE LONG POLE FOR 10lb PLUS, BY FISHING A SHORT HOOKLENGTH AND ·70g OLIVETTE RIG. IT'S AMAZING HOW HE CASTS SUCH A LIGHT RIG SO SMOOTHLY ON A LONG LINE AND 10 METRE TELESCOPIC POLE.

IT'S A VERY CLOSE MATCH, IN THE BALANCE RIGHT TO THE DEATH, BUT MY METHOD DID PROVE INVALUABLE FOR ESSEX COUNTY TEAM MATE STEVE OROURK WHOSE BAG OF 9lb WAS TOP WEIGHT.

RESULT: ESSEX COUNTY 21 · 15 · 8
COOKHAM 20 · 9 · 0

BULK SHOTTING HASN'T SOLVED THE PROBLEM EITHER. THE BLEAK ARE SIMPLY FOLLOWING THE BAIT DOWN AND MY FLOAT REFUSES TO SETTLE.

ONLY ONE THING FOR IT— I'VE DECIDED TO GET A BLEAK RIG OUT AND SEE WHAT KIND OF WEIGHT IS ON THE CARDS WITH THESE TINY FISH.

IGNESTI BLEAKER FLOAT

22 FINE BARBLESS

10 in 9½ oz HOOKLENGTH

GROUP OF Nº 11 SHOT

FEEDING HALF A DOZEN MAGGOTS EVERY CAST, I'M CATCHING PLENTY OF BLEAK ON A 6 METRE POLE, BUT I SUSPECT I COULD CATCH EVEN QUICKER CLOSER IN.

I'VE SHORTENED THE RIG DOWN TO JUST 3 METRES AND BY INTRODUCING A LITTLE CLOUDY GROUNDBAIT I'M REALLY 'BAGGING UP' AS FRANK BARLOW WOULD SAY...

... VAN DEN EYNDE ESSEX SKIPPER PETE CLAPPERTON HAS MOVED IN UPSTREAM.

...ENGLAND STAR BOB NUDD IS HERE

...AND THE 'RED MAN' JAN PORTER JUST STOPPED BY TO SAY HELLO.

I'VE TRIED MAGGOT ON A SHORT HOOKLENGTH BELOW AN OLIVETTE. THIS GETS THROUGH THE BLEAK BUT THE PRESENTATION ISN'T RIGHT.

OLIVETTE

10 in

NOW I'VE SET UP A LONG HOOKLENGTH WITH 3 STYLS SPREAD BELOW THE OLIVETTE. I'VE BEEN FEEDING HEMP, SO LET'S GIVE THIS A GO.

OLIVETTE

3 ft

SMALL STYLS

THE FLOAT DARTED UNDER FIRST TROT DOWN WITH A GRAIN OF HEMP ON THE HOOK, NOT A BAD SIZED FISH EITHER.

69

River Severn Continued

● Every barbel river in England appears to incite a similar record-breaking story. If all the reports are true, then salmon anglers have hooked record barbel on prawn or spinners from these waters during the Close Season. Just such a report circulated around the Severn — and there is every reason to believe it as double-figure specimens are on the increase.

A NICE ROACH.

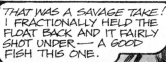

I'VE JUST SWITCHED TO HEMPSEED ON THE LONG POLE BELOW DIGLIS WEIR AT WORCESTER AND A GOOD FISH IS HOOKED.

FRANK 'BORIS' BARLOW IS FISHING HIS FAVOURITE STICK FLOAT. HE'S BEEN CATCHING CHUB, NOW A BARBEL HAS PICKED UP HIS BAIT.

THAT WAS A SAVAGE TAKE! I FRACTIONALLY HELD THE FLOAT BACK AND IT FAIRLY SHOT UNDER — A GOOD FISH THIS ONE.

OH YES! A CRACKING ROACH.

NEARLY 1½ lb THAT FISH AND I'M STRAIGHT INTO ANOTHER.

NO CHANCE! THE HOOK'S PULLED FREE.

TIME TO TRY THE FEEDER I THINK, PACKED WITH HEMP AND CASTER.

AUGUST
River Derwent
Borrowash, Derbyshire

I'VE BEEN LOOKING FORWARD TO THIS TRIP ON THE DERBYSHIRE DERWENT FOR A LONG TIME. I'M FISHING WITH MIDLANDS MATCHMAN JAN PORTER.

I'M ALSO FISHING LIGHT BELOW THE FLOAT—TWO № 11 SHOT BELOW A 3AAA INSERT WAGGLER. I TOOK A QUICK FLURRY OF SMALL CHUB ON CASTER, NOW I'M FINDING ROACH, MAINLY ON—THE—DROP.

20 KAMASAN WHISKER HOOK

NOW HE'S BACK ON THE FISHING SCENE WITH A VENGEANCE HAVING LED THE TRENTMEN SIDE TO DIVISION ONE SUCCESS ON THEIR HOME WATER.

THE DERWENT FISH SEEM TO WANT A LOT OF FEED. I'M REALLY STARTING TO BAG UP ON THE ROACH, FEEDING A HEMP AND CASTER MIX EVERY CAST AND FISHING SINGLE CASTER ON THE HOOK. I'M IGNORING ON—THE—DROP KNOCKS FROM SMALL STUFF AND LOOSE FEEDING _AFTER_ I'VE CAST OUT TO TRY AND GET THE BETTER ROACH DEEPER DOWN.

...AFTER ALL, IT'S NOT EVERY DAY YOU GET BRILLIANT ROACH SPORT LIKE THIS!

Angler's Mail

JAN SEEMS TO BE DRAWING UP STREAMS OF SMALL CHUB FROM THE SHALLOWS BELOW HIM. HE HAS DECIDED TO SWITCH FROM MAGGOTS TO HEMP AND CASTER TO SEE IF HE CAN LURE SOME LARGER FISH WHICH ARE PROBABLY SHOALED HERE AFTER SPAWNING.

JAN HAS PICKED A NOTED CHUB PEG ON THE RUN-IN TO SHALLOWS. MY PEG HAS A MUCH STEADIER FLOW FROM THE MIDDLE OUT AND MORE DEPTH ON THE INSIDE LINE — LOOKS GOOD FOR ROACH.

SHALLOWS

JAN'S USING ONE OF HIS OWN DESIGN MIDDY PEACOCK WAGGLERS...

...AND TO OVERCOME THICK BOTTOM WEED HE'S FISHING ON THE DROP.

21 90340 MUSTAD HOOK

STYL

STYL

STYL

STYL

STYL

FLOW

2 SWAN LOCKING SHOT

JAN'S TRADEMARK IN MATCH FISHING IS HIS COLOURFUL ALL-RED KIT. IT CERTAINLY DOESN'T SIGNAL DANGER TO THE FISH BECAUSE HE'S INTO SMALL CHUB ON MAGGOTS STRAIGHT AWAY! JAN GAVE UP FISHING FOR 6 YEARS TO PLAY LEAD GUITAR IN A ROCK GROUP.

THE CHUB ARE BOILING ON TOP IN JAN'S SWIM, SO HE LOOSE FEEDS MAGGOTS BEFORE CASTING TO LAND HIS BAITED HOOK AMONG THE EAGER FISH. IF HE CARRIES ON LIKE THIS JAN IS GOING TO GET AN IMPRESSIVE WEIGHT.

I'M GETTING THE ODD CHUB, BUT I DON'T THINK THERE ARE MANY IN THIS SWIM. IF I HAD STARTED ON MAGGOT I THINK I WOULD HAVE DRAWN A FEW MORE FISH UP FROM JAN'S SWIM, BUT I'LL STICK WITH THE ROACH ON CASTER...

WELL THAT'S EXTRAORDINARY! THE FISH HAVE DISAPPEARED AS SOON AS THE HEMP AND CASTER WENT IN!

WHILE JAN SORTS OUT THAT ALARMING PROBLEM I'M SETTING UP A MIDDY PETE WARREN STICK FLOAT TO SEE IF I CAN BRING THE ROACH IN EVEN CLOSER.

River Derwent Continued

● Jan Porter's striking all-red kit is unique in angling but matching luggage and jackets bearing the names of sponsors have become all the rage in team fishing. Meanwhile, sombre colours remain standard issue in specimen hunting where camouflage rather than eye-catching colours are the priority.

AUGUST
Lodge Pool
Farnham, Surrey

I'M GOING TO FISH THE WAGGLER AND BOMB, USING A MARKER LEFT BY A CARP ANGLER FOR MY FAR LINE FEEDING.

THIS SECLUDED DAY TICKET LAKE IN HAMPSHIRE LIES ON FORESTRY COMMISSION LAND AND IS CONTROLLED BY THE LOCAL FARNHAM CLUB. IT HOLDS PLENTY OF CARP, ROACH AND BREAM, BUT SPORT HAS BEEN VERY UNPREDICTABLE AND I DON'T KNOW WHAT TO EXPECT. THE SWIM I'VE CHOSEN IS AT THE POPULAR DAM END.

THERE'S SOME BIG CARP MOVING UNDER THE COVER TO MY LEFT, BUT NONE OF THE CARP ANGLERS HAVE HAD A RUN IN THE BRIGHT, WINDLESS CONDITIONS.

THAT DIDN'T TAKE TOO LONG. THE WATER IS QUITE COLOURED BUT I'M GETTING BITES QUICKLY ON CASTER — MUST BE A LOT OF FISH IN HERE.

I DON'T UNDERSTAND THIS. DESPITE PILING IN THE FEED I'M STILL NOT ATTRACTING ANY OF THE BIGGER FISH — EVEN THE SMALL ROACH ARE FADING FAST.

I'VE GIVEN THE FISH PLENTY OF TIME TO SETTLE ON THE FAR LINE SO LET'S TRY THE LEGER...

...LOOK AT THAT! — THE QUIVERTIP HARDLY HAD TIME TO SETTLE AND IT SOARED ROUND.

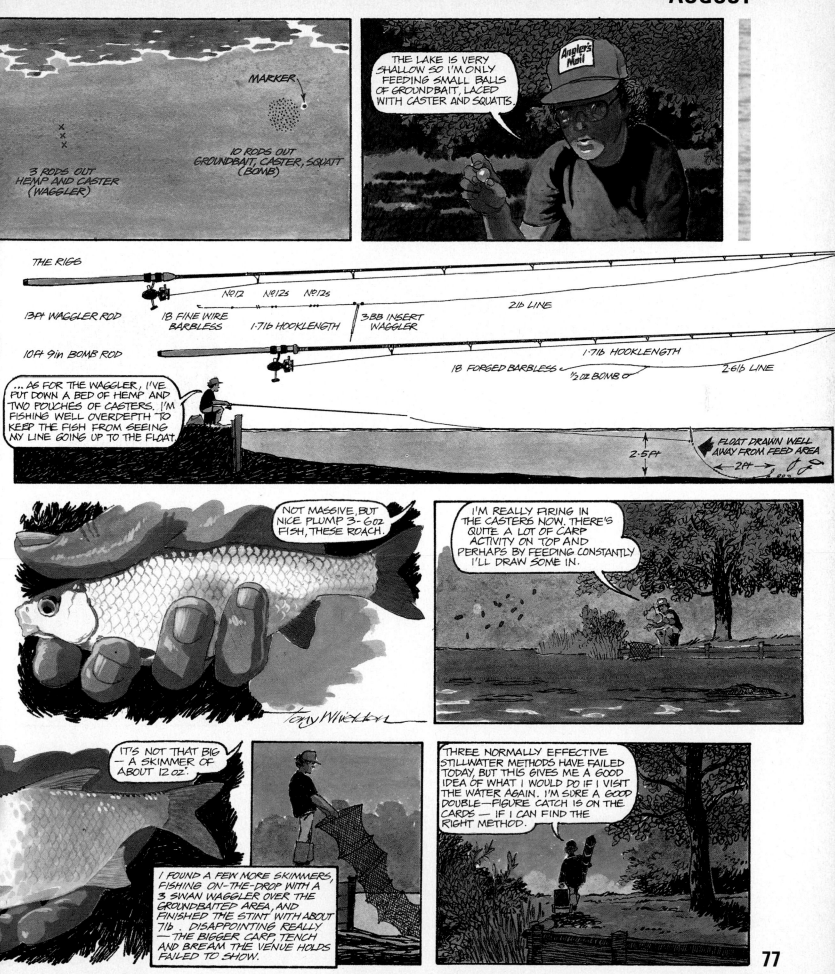

MARKER

10 RODS OUT
GROUNDBAIT, CASTER, SQUATT
(BOMB)

3 RODS OUT
HEMP AND CASTER
(WAGGLER)

THE LAKE IS VERY
SHALLOW SO I'M ONLY
FEEDING SMALL BALLS
OF GROUNDBAIT, LACED
WITH CASTER AND SQUATTS.

THE RIGS

13ft WAGGLER ROD

Nº12 Nº12s Nº12s   2lb LINE

18 FINE WIRE   1·7lb HOOKLENGTH   3BB INSERT
BARBLESS   WAGGLER

10ft 9in BOMB ROD

1·7lb HOOKLENGTH

18 FORGED BARBLESS   ½ OZ BOMB   2·6lb LINE

...AS FOR THE WAGGLER, I'VE
PUT DOWN A BED OF HEMP AND
TWO POUCHES OF CASTERS. I'M
FISHING WELL OVERDEPTH TO
KEEP THE FISH FROM SEEING
MY LINE GOING UP TO THE FLOAT.

FLOAT DRAWN WELL
AWAY FROM FEED AREA

2·5ft   2ft

NOT MASSIVE, BUT
NICE PLUMP 3- 6oz
FISH, THESE ROACH.

I'M REALLY FIRING IN
THE CASTERS NOW. THERE'S
QUITE A LOT OF CARP
ACTIVITY ON TOP AND
PERHAPS BY FEEDING CONSTANTLY
I'LL DRAW SOME IN.

Tony Whieldon

IT'S NOT THAT BIG
— A SKIMMER OF
ABOUT 12 OZ.

I FOUND A FEW MORE SKIMMERS,
FISHING ON-THE-DROP WITH A
3 SWAN WAGGLER OVER THE
GROUNDBAITED AREA, AND
FINISHED THE STINT WITH ABOUT
7lb. DISAPPOINTING REALLY
— THE BIGGER CARP, TENCH
AND BREAM THE VENUE HOLDS
FAILED TO SHOW.

THREE NORMALLY EFFECTIVE
STILLWATER METHODS HAVE FAILED
TODAY, BUT THIS GIVES ME A GOOD
IDEA OF WHAT I WOULD DO IF I VISIT
THE WATER AGAIN. I'M SURE A GOOD
DOUBLE-FIGURE CATCH IS ON THE
CARDS — IF I CAN FIND THE
RIGHT METHOD.

SEPTEMBER
Royalty Fishery
Hampshire Avon, Christchurch

THE PARLOUR IS PROBABLY THE MOST FAMOUS SWIM ON THE HAMPSHIRE AVON'S ROYALTY FISHERY AT CHRISTCHURCH. THE POOL IS OFTEN FULL OF SALMON FRESH IN FROM THE SEA AND CONTAINS AT LEAST ONE BARBEL ESTIMATED AT 14lb AS WELL AS 3lb ROACH AND HUGE CHUB. YOU CAN'T FISH BEYOND THE CHAIN AND THAT'S WHERE MOST OF THE MONSTERS HIDE UP — THEY SWIM UNDER THE APRON, ALMOST BENEATH THE BUILDING ITSELF.

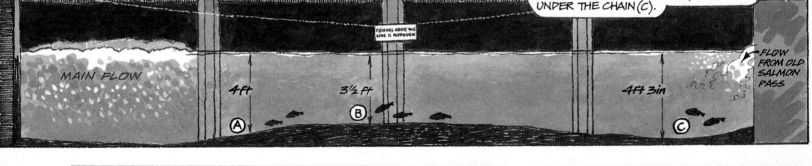

MOST OF THE FLOW IS COMING THROUGH ON THE FAR SIDE. I FANCY THERE COULD BE FISH JUST OFF THIS (A). THERE'S ALSO A NICE FLAT AREA IN THE CENTRE OF THE POOL — I'LL TRY HERE TO START WITH (B). MY PLUMMET ALSO TELLS ME THERE'S AN INTERESTING SPOT CLOSER IN, TO MY RIGHT, UNDER THE CHAIN (C).

FISHING ABOVE THIS LINE IS FORBIDDEN

MAIN FLOW

4ft

3½ ft

4ft 3in

FLOW FROM OLD SALMON PASS

Ⓐ   Ⓑ   Ⓒ

MY FIRST FISH WAS A 1lb CHUB

ON THE FAR BANK, BELOW A WILLOW, RAY'S STARTED SEARCHING OUT THE WEEDY RUNS WITH LARGE CHUNKS OF LUNCHEON MEAT. HE USES 10lb STRAIGHT THROUGH TO A SIZE 2 LION D'OR HOOK.

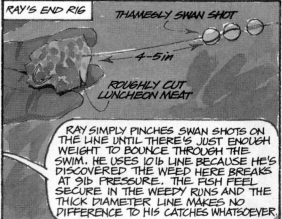

RAY'S END RIG

THAMESLY SWAN SHOT

4-5in

ROUGHLY CUT LUNCHEON MEAT

RAY SIMPLY PINCHES SWAN SHOTS ON THE LINE UNTIL THERE'S JUST ENOUGH WEIGHT TO BOUNCE THROUGH THE SWIM. HE USES 10lb LINE BECAUSE HE'S DISCOVERED THE WEED HERE BREAKS AT 9lb PRESSURE. THE FISH FEEL SECURE IN THE WEEDY RUNS AND THE THICK DIAMETER LINE MAKES NO DIFFERENCE TO HIS CATCHES WHATSOEVER.

MY COMPANION, RAY WALTON OF THE BARBEL CATCHERS, IS GOING TO FISH THE WEED-CHOKED STRETCH, BETWEEN THE PARLOUR AND THE MAIN RIVER, WHICH MOST ANGLERS WOULDN'T GIVE A SECOND GLANCE.
RAY HAS BEEN RESEARCHING THE ROYALTY BARBEL FOR SIX YEARS AND WAS RESPONSIBLE FOR EXPOSING THE PHENOMENON OF EXTRA WHISKERS. HE VIRTUALLY KNOWS EVERY SINGLE SPECIMEN ON THE ROYALTY BY SIGHT.

RAY'S KIT

A. TINS OF LUNCHEON MEAT— He uses four tins a session.

B. WATER PH KIT.

C. BINOCULARS.

D. WALKIE TALKIES.

E. CAMERA.

F. FRIARS BALSAM—which Ray brushes on sores or other damage on barbel — it helps them heal remarkably quickly.

G. AIR THERMOMETER.

H. WATER THERMOMETER

I. TAPE RECORDER — for making notes.

J. MEASURING TAPE.

K. SCALES.

No.8
No.8
No.1s SANDVIK
LIGNUM STICK
No.8 1·7lb
18 FORGED BARBLESS

I THINK THESE PARLOUR FISH MUST SEE A LOT OF SPECIMEN GEAR. LET'S SEE HOW THEY RESPOND TO THE LIGHT APPROACH AND LOTS OF CASTERS.

I'M USING SANDVIK BULK SHOT IN CASE I GET A BIG FISH CHARGING OFF DOWNSTREAM INTO THE WEED. THESE WILL THEN POP OFF THE LINE LESSENING THE RISK OF A BREAK.

BY AIMING MY CATAPULT LOW I CAN GET THE BULK OF MY CASTERS IN THE MIDDLE, BUT THIS MAKES A FEW SKIM ACROSS THE SURFACE TOWARDS THE MAIN INFLUX OF WATER. THIS GIVES ME A GOOD AREA TO WORK WITH MY FLOAT TACKLE.

WEED
FLOW
FLOW — PATH OF FLOAT
ODD CASTERS FALL HERE
MAIN FEED

SOMETHING'S SNAPPED UP MY DOUBLE CASTER, OFFERING RIGHT AWAY!

RAY HOLDS HIS ROD ALL THE TIME, FEELING FOR BITES THROUGH THE LINE. HE LETS SLACK LINE REST ON THE WEED NOW AND THEN TO HOLD THE BAIT STILL — THEN TWITCHES IT SO THAT IT MOVES ON DOWN THE SWIM.

BACK AT THE POOL

I'VE HIT INTO SOMETHING BIG!

Royalty Fishery Continued

● Ray Walton's researches into barbel prove that some individuals travel long distances in a short space of time and by no means stay put in the area where they were first hooked. This nomadic tendency may be the result of angling pressure which is intense in some Avon swims where well known heavyweights are in residence.

DAMN! THE FISH JUST TOUCHED THE WEED AND I FELT THE HOOK PULL OUT.

I'VE BEEN PLAYING THIS FISH FOR SEVERAL MINUTES ON THE PARLOUR POOL ON THE HAMPSHIRE AVON AT CHRISTCHURCH. IT'S DARTING ALL OVER THE PLACE! SUDDENLY IT LIFTS IN THE WATER AND I SEE IT'S A COMMON CARP OF ABOUT 7 lb! IT'S TRYING TO GET INTO THE WEED TO MY LEFT NOW — I'M PILING ON THE SIDESTRAIN.

RAY INFORMS ME THE BARBEL WAS 4½ lb — THESE WALKIE-TALKIES ARE BRILLIANT WHEN YOU'RE FISHING WITH COMPANY. I THINK I'LL POP DOWN AND SEE HOW RAY IS FINDING THE BARBEL — THAT'S AFTER I'VE LANDED THIS NICE 2 lb PLUS CHUB.

.... THEN RETURNS TO RUN THE BAIT THROUGH AGAIN. OFTEN HE FINDS A FISH THAT'S MISSED THE MEAL THE FIRST TIME, OR HAS BEEN SUSPICIOUS, DOESN'T LET HIS BAIT GO UNNOTICED NEXT TIME AROUND.

EVEN WITH QUITE A BIT OF SLACK IN THE LINE, SLIGHT PLUCKS FROM INTERESTED FISH ARE FELT QUITE POSITIVELY. *THAT WAS A KNOCK!*

RAY RECKONS MANY ANGLERS IGNORE SLIGHT KNOCKS LIKE THAT, THINKING THEY'RE CAUSED BY SMALL FISH, BUT HE KNOWS DIFFERENTLY. HE PRICKED A GOOD FISH THERE!

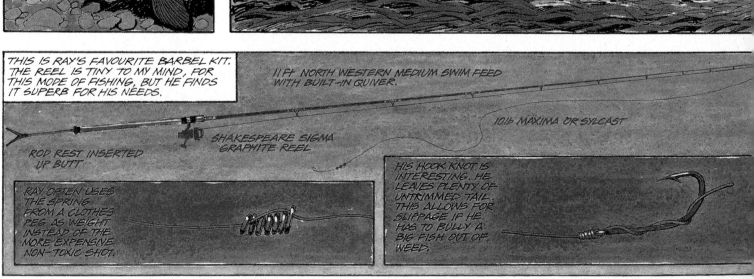

THIS IS RAY'S FAVOURITE BARBEL KIT. THE REEL IS TINY TO MY MIND, FOR THIS MODE OF FISHING, BUT HE FINDS IT SUPERB FOR HIS NEEDS.

11 Ft NORTH WESTERN MEDIUM SWIM FEED WITH BUILT-IN QUIVER.

10 lb MAXIMA OR SYLCAST

ROD REST INSERTED UP BUTT

SHAKESPEARE SIGMA GRAPHITE REEL

RAY OFTEN USES THE SPRING FROM A CLOTHES PEG AS WEIGHT INSTEAD OF THE MORE EXPENSIVE NON-TOXIC SHOT.

HIS HOOK KNOT IS INTERESTING.. HE LEAVES PLENTY OF UNTRIMMED TAIL. THIS ALLOWS FOR SLIPPAGE IF HE HAS TO BULLY A BIG FISH OUT OF WEED.

Royalty Fishery Continued

● Considerable controversy surrounds Ray Walton's discovery of the extra whiskers sprouted by many barbel on rivers as far apart as the Lea and Hampshire Avon. Some claim the phenomenon is not new but Ray is adamant that it demonstrates all is not well with their diet or possibly water quality.

WHAT A LOVELY FISH. RAY'S WEIGHED IT FOR ME AT 8lb 3oz — NOT BAD FOR AN 18 HOOK AND 1·7lb HOOKLENGTH!

I'VE BEEN PLAYING THIS FISH IN THE PARLOUR FOR 3 OR 4 MINUTES NOW.

I THINK IT'S A BIG BARBEL— IT'S A LOT SLOWER MOVING THAN THAT CARP I LOST.

YES IT'S A BARBEL— AND BY THE LOOKS OF IT MY PAN LANDING NET IS BARELY BIG ENOUGH.

I'M GETTING PLENTY OF BITES CLOSE IN TO MY BANK. I GET A RESPONSE IN THE SLACK OR IF I DRAG THE FLOAT ACROSS THE WATER FLOWING OUT FROM THE SALMON PASS.

FLOW
FLOAT
SLACK

HERE'S ANOTHER GOOD FISH....

....A SUPERBLY CONDITIONED 4lb CHUB.

THAT'S ANNOYING. THE HOOK'S GONE. IT'S STRANGE BECAUSE MY TACKLE HAS BEEN STANDING UP TO THE OCCASION SO FAR. MIND YOU, I HAD TIED ON A NEW PATTERN I'D BEEN ASKED TO TRY OUT FOR REVIEWING PURPOSES.

LET'S HAVE A LOOK AT ANOTHER. NO WONDER— THE SPADES ON THESE ARE LIKE RAZORS! THAT LITTLE LOT CAN GO STRAIGHT IN THE BIN. NO REVIEW FOR THIS PRODUCT— THE SUPPLIER MIGHT WELL GET A STIFF LETTER THOUGH.

THIS IS BETTER. BACK TO MY OLD FAVOURITES AND NO PROBLEMS. STILL YOU'VE GOT TO BE FAIR AND TRY NEW PRODUCTS. I ONLY WISH A LITTLE MORE THOUGHT WENT INTO SOME OF THEM.

SEPTEMBER
Exeter Canal
Lime Kilns, Devon

A MATCH WAS WON ON PERMANENT PEG 119 — BY THE SEWAGE BARGE — BUT WE FANCY THESE WIDER SWIMS IN FRONT OF THE CAR PARK.

I'VE GOT ROB ROYCE OF BRIDGWATER WITH ME TODAY. HE WON A COMPETITION, EARLIER IN THE YEAR, TO APPEAR IN MY DIARY AND WE'VE DECIDED ON A SESSION AT THE LIME KILN STRETCH OF THE EXETER CANAL. ROB'S HOME WATERS IN SOMERSET ARE THE BRIDGWATER CANAL AND HUNTSPILL. HE'LL FIND THIS VENUE A LOT DEEPER. I LIKE HIS HAT!

TO RING THE CHANGES LATER ON I'VE SET UP A LONG POLE RIG TO FISH 14 ft DEEP. I'LL FLICK SOME HEMP AND MAGGOTS OUT REGULARLY AND TRY THE POLE AT ODD INTERVALS TO SEE IF ANYTHING MOVES IN.

IT DIDN'T TAKE LONG FOR A BITE, BUT THAT'S THE ONLY TROUBLE WITH SMALL BAITS — A TINY PERCH HAS SNAPPED UP THE OFFERING.

THAT'S A BETTER ONE! A COUPLE OF TINY TWITCHES ON THE QUIVERTIP AND I STRIKE INTO A PLEASING 12 oz SKIMMER.

I'M USING MY SLACK LINE TECHNIQUE NOW — LETTING THE LINE BOW INTO THE DRIFT TO SEE IF THIS DRAWS A MORE POSITIVE TAKE.

MEANWHILE BOB'S STRUGGLING. HE'S TRIED THE SWINGTIP AND THE WAGGLER BUT ONLY HAD A SMALL PERCH SO FAR.

AS FOR ME I'M HITTING INTO SKIMMER AFTER SKIMMER.

BARGE   BARGE

I'LL START ON THE OPEN-END FEEDER. IT'S VERY WEEDY ON THE FAR BANK SO I'LL CONCENTRATE JUST PAST THE MIDDLE WHERE IT SEEMS CLEARER. I'M HOPING TO FIND THE LIME KILN'S SKIMMERS.

18 in loop   1lb hooklength

3lb reel line   American link swivel   Bead   Cage feeder   20 Whisker barb

1 Gram wire stem bodied pole float

1.5 Main line

Olivette

Styl
9½ oz hooklength
Styl

22 series 4 Tubertini

MY HOOKBAIT IS TWO PINKIES WHICH ARE NICE AND SOFT — SKIMMERS TAKE THEM WELL. IN THE FEEDER, I'VE PACKED A MIXTURE OF HEMP, CASTERS AND SQUATTS IN A MINIMUM OF SOFT GROUNDBAIT. THE SQUATTS WILL PULL ANYTHING AROUND WHILE THE CASTERS WILL HOLD ANY BETTER FISH.

YES! WITH LESS RESISTANCE THE TIP WENT ROUND.

A BETTER SKIMMER, JUST OVER THE POUND MARK.

I'VE GOT THE FEEDER MIX JUST RIGHT. THE FEED'S COMING OUT AS THE FEEDER HITS ...

..AND THE SKIMMERS ARE HOMING IN ON-THE-DROP. NINE SKIMMERS UP TO A POUND IN THE NET ALREADY.

Exeter Canal Continued

● The wide and deep reaches of the Exeter Canal have become familiar to matchmen throughout the country as a popular Close Season series has been promoted on the water in recent years. The Lime Kilns is now nationally known for its bream potential.

MAIL READER ROB ROYCE IS FISHING WITH ME ON THE EXETER CANAL, BUT HIS SWIM ISN'T PRODUCING THE GOODS....

I THINK THE GENTLE LOOSE FEEDING WASN'T POSITIVE ENOUGH IN THIS DEPTH OF WATER. I WAS GETTING ODD KNOCKS ON THE DROP— NOW I'VE CONCENTRATED THE FISH ON THE BOTTOM AND THEY'RE REALLY SNAPPING UP MY SINGLE MAGGOT HOOKBAIT.

I'M STILL GETTING BITES FROM THE ROACH ON-THE-DROP BY LOOSE FEEDING MAGGOTS OVER THE GROUNDBAIT, BUT THE FISH ARE A LOT DEEPER DOWN AND I'M CONNECTING WELL.

THIS IS A BETTER FISH IT'S PULLING A FAIR BIT OF ELASTIC FROM THE TIP OF MY POLE. I MANAGED TO AVOID A BITE ON-THE-DROP THAT TIME AND SETTLED MY HOOKBAIT ON THE BOTTOM FOR A COUPLE OF MINUTES.

ROB'S BEEN TRYING SOME OF MY GROUNDBAIT MIX IN HIS FEEDER AND FINALLY GETS A BITE, BUT THE EXCITEMENT IS SHORT LIVED — IT'S ONLY A TINY BOOTLACE EEL!

I EXPERIMENT BY SHORTENING MY RIG BUT IT ONLY BRINGS SMALL ROACH.

BACK HARD ON THE BOTTOM AGAIN AND THE BREAM ARE READY AND WAITING.

River Thames Continued

● Heavy boat traffic in summer poses problems for anglers right along the Thames and at weekends it can become unbearable. The congestion is unlikely to ease and the need to develop stillwater venues exclusively for fishing is now regarded by many in the sport as the only salvation. Luckily, there are many hundreds of acres of pits in the Thames Valley where you can escape.

AFTER TAKING THREE CHUB IN QUICK SUCCESSION, THE PLEASURE BOATS INTERRUPT MATTERS. THAT'S THE TROUBLE WITH THIS LONG RANGE FEEDER METHOD — YOU SOMETIMES HAVE TO WAIT SEVERAL MINUTES BEFORE RECASTING BECAUSE OF BOAT TRAFFIC.

THE BOATS TEND TO PUSH THE FISH TIGHTER IN TO THE FAR BANK, BUT ON THE OTHER HAND THE REST CAN DO THE SWIM GOOD. ON BALANCE IT'S BETTER TO SIT IT OUT WITHOUT A BAIT IN THE WATER BECAUSE IF A PROPELLER CATCHES THE LINE IT COULD ALMOST EMPTY THE SPOOL.

THE APPEARANCE OF THE PERCH IS FOLLOWED BY A STRANGE LULL — I WONDER WHAT'S HAPPENED TO THE CHUB?

A FEEDER CRAMMED WITH FLOATING MAGGOTS BROUGHT THE FISH BACK STRAIGHT AWAY. THERE'S NO DOUBT IN MY MIND THAT FLOATERS CAN TRANSFORM A SWIM — THE RUSE HAS WORKED MANY TIMES ON THIS STRETCH OF THE RIVER, AND ELSEWHERE.

Tony Whieldon

I LOST THAT FISH TOO, SO I'M GOING TO TRY RAISING THE ROD ABOVE MY HEAD TO GET THIS ONE OVER THE SNAG.

THAT'S BETTER. THE CHUB STAYED UP IN THE WATER AND I'VE GOT IT TO THE NET.

MY TWO BEST FISH ARE A POUND PLUS PERCH AND THE 3lb CHUB. AFTER THREE HOURS I'M WELL ON MY WAY TO 20lb, WITH EIGHT CHUB ALTOGETHER. UNFORTUNATELY I'VE GOT TO LEAVE NOW, JUST WHEN THE FISH ARE LINING UP.
BUT THAT'S LIFE!

River Lea Continued

● There's a great irony attached to this story of Dave's session in the sunken barge swim. He returned to the same spot a few days later and found no sign of the wreckage on the far bank. It had been removed – presumably by British Waterways – and with it had gone the chub shoals!

NOVEMBER
Private Fenland Drains
Cambridgeshire

DR. BARRIE RICKARDS OF CAMBRIDGE UNIVERSITY TRAVELS THE WORLD AS ONE OF THE U.K'S TOP GEOLOGISTS, BUT HIS FIRST HOME IS THE CAMBRIDGESHIRE FENS WHERE HE HUNTS FOR PIKE AND ZANDER AT EVERY OPPORTUNITY. JUST AFTER FIRST LIGHT THIS MORNING, DAVE COSTER AND I MET UP WITH BARRIE ON A PRIVATE, NARROW DRAIN WHERE HE IS CONFIDENT OF SOME PIKE ACTION BEFORE 10 a.m.

BY 9 a.m. IT'S OBVIOUS THIS IS GOING TO BE A TOUGH DAY. BARRIE RECKONS THE REAL CULPRIT IS AN OVERNIGHT LOW PRESSURE FRONT WHICH MOVED QUICKLY ACROSS THE COUNTRY. THAT USUALLY SPELLS CURTAINS FOR BAIT FISHING IN ITS IMMEDIATE AFTERMATH, BUT LURES OFTEN PRODUCE UNDER THESE CONDITIONS SO HE RIGS UP HIS 5 Ft AMERICAN BAITCASTING ROD WITH A MINI MULTIPLIER AND SHAKESPEARE BIG S PLUG. LAST WEEK HE HAD A 24 POUNDER ON THIS OUTFIT!

HERE'S JUST A SMALL SELECTION OF BARRIE'S LURES. THE SHAKESPEARE PLUGS INCLUDE THE BIG S AND RED AND SILVER POPPER. THERE ARE THREE VARIANTS OF THE NORWICH SPOON AND THE SPINNER SELECTION INCLUDES THE NEW KILKO WITH BLUE BARS. THE JOINTED PLUG ON THE LEFT IS A KWIKFISH K 12. LURES MUST BE FISHED ON A COUPLE OF WIRE TRACES FOR SECURITY. SOMETIMES IT HELPS TO ADD A WYE LEAD AT THE HEAD OF THE TRACE WITH SPINNERS.

THE NEWS FROM DAVE'S SWIM ISN'T GOOD. HE HAS NETTED A SMALL RUDD BUT RECKONS HE'D BETTER GO HOME BEFORE HE CATCHES PNEUMONIA! AS HE TRUDGES OVER THE FIELDS TO HIS CAR, BARRIE LANDS ANOTHER JACK. BY LATE DECEMBER WHEN ALL THE WEED HAS DIED BACK, THERE'LL BE NO SIGN OF JACKS. ALL OF THEM WILL BE INSIDE MUCH BIGGER PIKE. SUDDENLY THE PUMP AT THE HEAD OF THE DRAIN STARTS UP — IT'S TIME TO GO.

WE THROW THE RODS IN THE BACK OF THE CAR AND SWITCH TO A KNOWN HOTSPOT FOR DOUBLES ON THE GREAT OUSE RELIEF CHANNEL. IT IS NOW 11 a.m. AND POURING WITH RAIN. THIS TIME BARRIE TRIES A MACKEREL TAIL AS WELL AS A SMELT. THE WIND THREATENS TO BLOW HIS RODS CLEAN OFF THE OPTONICS SO HE SECURES THEM WITH ELASTIC BANDS. HE STILL LIKES USING WASHING-UP BOTTLE TOPS TO SIGNAL DROP-BACKS AND INSERTS A STARLITE IN PLASTIC TUBING FOR SESSIONS AFTER DARK. WE SIT UNDER THE BROLLY FOR MORE THAN TWO HOURS WITHOUT A RUN. — THIS IS GETTING DESPERATE.

STARLITE

APPEARANCES ARE DECEPTIVE ON THESE TINY DRAINS. MANY OF THEM HOLD ENORMOUS STOCKS OF QUALITY BREAM AND ROACH WHICH GROW FAT IN THE ENRICHED WEEDY WATERS. PIKE ALSO PACK ON WEIGHT VERY QUICKLY AS THEY DON'T HAVE TO MOVE VERY FAR TO GRAB A SATISFYING SNACK, BUT YOU'VE GOT TO STAY OFF THE SKYLINE WHICH IS EASIER SAID THAN DONE ON THESE STEEP SIDED BANKS. BARRIE HAS DUG OUT A COUPLE OF SWIMS AND SETTLES INTO A FAVOURITE SPOT WHERE THERE'S 6FT OF WATER IN MID-CHANNEL.

BARRIE HAS JUST SIGNED UP AS A SHAKESPEARE CONSULTANT AND IMMEDIATELY BAGGED A COUPLE OF THEIR THREE-PIECE EQUALISER RODS FOR HIS DEADBAIT FISHING. THEY ARE 3lb TEST CURVE BEASTS BUT BARRIE RECKONS THEY'VE GOT A SMASHING ACTION. HIS REELS ARE OLD, TRUSTY MITCHELLS AND THE LINE IS 12lb PLATIL. HE'S FISHING TWO RODS — ONE LEGER AND THE OTHER FLOAT — WITH SMELT DEADBAITS. ALTHOUGH THERE IS STILL A LOT OF BOTTOM WEED, THE PIKE SHOULD SOON SNIFF OUT THESE STRONG SMELLING FISH NO MATTER HOW FESTOONED THEY GET.

BARRIE'S DEADBAIT RIG

- BILLY LANE STOP KNOT
- BEAD
- SLIDING PILOT FLOAT
- 12lb PLATIL MAIN LINE
- BEAD
- SNAPLINK SWIVEL
- SWIVEL
- 3/4 OZ BOMB
- UPPER WIRE TRACE 10-12 in.
- SNAPLINK SWIVEL
- SIZE 8 TREBLES
- SLIDING RYDER HOOK

MEANWHILE, DAVE HAS SET UP IN A RAKED SWIM ABOUT 40 YARDS AWAY BUT HE'S NOT A HAPPY MAN. HE IS SUFFERING FROM A SEVERE HEAD COLD AND STRONG WINDS SWEEPING ACROSS THE FENS ARE NOT DOING HIM ANY GOOD AT ALL. THERE WAS ALSO AN OMINOUS TEMPERATURE DROP OVERNIGHT WHICH HAS CHILLED THE WATER AND THERE SEEMS LITTLE CHANCE OF THE BREAM FEEDING TODAY. DAVE IMMEDIATELY GOES ON PUNCHED BREAD IN THE HOPE OF SOME ROACH BUT HIS SWIM IS UNRESPONSIVE.

AFTER WORKING HIS WAY ALONG THE EDGE OF THE DRAIN FLICKING OUT THE PLUG IN FRONT OF HIM, BARRIE SWITCHES TO A BIG SPOON — THE RESULT IS A JACK PIKE WHICH ISN'T MUCH LONGER THAN THE LURE!

THE SAME TERMINAL SET-UP IS ALSO USED FOR LEGER RIGS — WITH THE BOMB SOMETIMES FIXED ON THE SNAPLINK.

ANOTHER CHANGE OF SCENERY! AT 2 p.m. WE SHOOT OVER TO THE DELPH TO WORK LURES THROUGH A ONE MILE STRETCH WHICH IS ABSOLUTELY SOLID WITH PIKE. IF WE DON'T GET A DOUBLE HERE THEN IT'S OBVIOUS THE WHOLE OF THE FENS HAS TURNED OFF. THE RAIN IS DRIVING INTO OUR FACES BUT WE RESOLUTELY FLASH AN ASSORTMENT OF SPOONS AND PLUGS THROUGH EVERY YARD OF WATER.

THAT'S THE NEAREST WE'VE COME TODAY! A FISH OF AROUND 8 lb FOLLOWS BARRIE'S SPOON ALL THE WAY TO THE BANK ONLY TO TURN AWAY AT THE LAST SECOND. IT WAS THE ONLY SIGN OF LIFE IN THE STRETCH. WE'RE BOTH SOAKED BUT WE'RE NOT BEATEN YET.

OUR LAST HOPE IS ANOTHER TINY DRAIN WHERE THE PIKE ARE USUALLY SUCKERS FOR A FLASHY SPOON. YOU'VE GOT TO ADMIRE BARRIE'S PERSISTENCE ON A DAY WHEN THE ODDS ARE TOTALLY STACKED AGAINST HIM. AT 4.30 p.m. WE ADMIT DEFEAT JUST AS THE SKIES CLEAR FOR THE FIRST TIME. THE WEAK WINTERY SUN RAISES OUR SPIRITS AND REMINDS US THAT TOMORROW COULD BE AS DIFFERENT AGAIN.

RAHAM SMITH

IV'E ONLY SET UP A LIGHT FEEDER RIG AND A SHORT POLE. THE WIND IS NEARING STORM FORCE. ANY OTHER METHODS ARE GOING TO BE IMPOSSIBLE TO CONTROL. IVE STARTED ON THE FEEDER WHILE I TRY TO BUILD UP THE INSIDE POLE LINE.

I'M USING A TARGET BOARD WITH A QUIVERTIP. IT'S GOING TO BE HARD ENOUGH TO SPOT BITES IN THIS DREADFUL WIND AND THE BOARD MIGHT JUST MAKE THE DIFFERENCE.

I'M GOING TO LENGTHEN MY HOOKLENGTH AND SCALE DOWN TO A 22 HOOK WITH DOUBLE RED PINKIE. A DRIER MIX IN MY CAGE FEEDER WILL ALSO GET MORE CLOUD INTO THE SWIM.

TWO HOURS INTO THE MATCH AND I'M NOW TRYING THE SHORT POLE "TO HAND" STYLE, BUT EVEN THIS IS DIFFICULT IN THIS WIND.

GRAHAM'S JUST KEPT SMALL HELPINGS OF LOOSE MAGGOTS GOING IN — HE COULD BE INTO DOUBLE FIGURES NOW. FOR ME THOUGH IT'S BEEN A RIGHT GRUELLER— ONLY ABOUT 4lb OF SKIMMERS.

RESULTS
1st. GRAHAM SMITH (Tottenham) 13·6·0
2nd. MELVIN REEVES (Stevenage) 9·3·0
3rd. STEVE TYLER (Poplett) 9·2·0

NOVEMBER
Grand Union Canal
Watford, Hertfordshire

KEY TO LADY CAPELS HOTSPOTS

1. SWIM BELOW HUNTON BRIDGE LOCK. MATCH-WINNING PEG. HAS PRODUCED MANY 2lb ROACH, BREAM TO 6lb, CHUB TO 4lb.

2. SEWERAGE OUTLET. TENCH SHOW HERE IN SUMMER.

3. NARROWS ABOVE HUNTON BRIDGE WIDES. NO COVER ON FAR BANK BUT SUPERB SKIMMER HOLDING SPOT.

4. UPPER WIDES. HOLDS BIG ROACH, CARP, SKIMMERS AND ONE SHOAL OF BIG BREAM.

5. MOTORWAY BRIDGE. GOOD CHUB PEG, BUT A BIT HIT OR MISS.

6. DEAD WATER. THROWS UP ODD GOOD WEIGHTS OF CHUB AND BREAM. CARP TO 14lb LIVE HERE.

7. MOUTH OF BACKSTREAM. TOP CHUB AND ROACH SWIM.

8. SHALLOWS. OVERGROWN FAR BANK HOLDS BIG CHUB. QUALITY ROACH SHOW DOWN MIDDLE TO LONG POLE. FAVOURED DRAW.

9. LADY CAPELS WIDES. THE 5 PEGS HERE ARE EVERY MATCHMAN'S DREAM DRAW, CAPABLE OF TURNING UP BIG WEIGHTS OF CHUB, BREAM, ROACH, CARP.

10. SCHOOLHOUSE BEND. FAR BANK TREE COVER HOLDS LOTS OF CHUB AND CARP.

11. RUSH BED. FULL OF CARP AND CHUB. A HEARTBREAK — DIFFICULT TO GET FISH OUT.

12. WHITE BRIDGE. CANAL NARROWS. CHUB AND ROACH ALWAYS RESIDENT.

13. CATTLE DRINK. GREAT ROACH PEG.

14. BOOM. BEST CHUB SWIM ON VENUE. HAS WON MORE MATCHES THAN ANY OTHER SWIM.

15. DEAD POUND. GOOD DRAW WHEN CANAL IS CARRYING EXTRA WATER. TURNS UP CHUB, SKIMMERS, ROACH AND GUDGEON. SOMETIMES WINS WINTER MATCHES.

16. GUDGEON ALLEY. FULL OF GUDGEON AND MINNOWS. ONE SWIM HAS A BUSH ON FAR BANK. THIS ALWAYS HOLDS BIG CHUB AND IS OFTEN A WINNING DRAW.

LADY CAPELS HOTSPOTS

Hemel Hempstead

HUNTON BRIDGE

HUNTON LOCK

SEWERAGE OUTLET

HUNTON BRIDGE WIDES

RUSHES

MOTORWAY BRIDGE

BACKSTREAM

DEAD POUND

LOCK

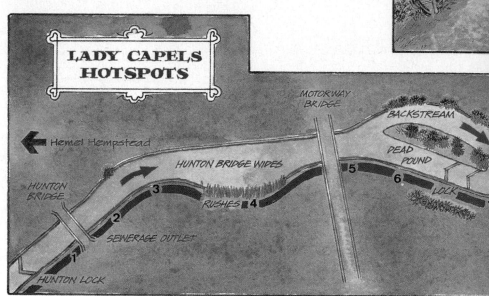

SLACK WATER

MAIN FLOW

A

B

I'VE EXPLORED AROUND THE FAR-BANK TREES AND ALONG THE WALL AT THE BOTTOM OF THE GARDENS, BUT ONLY SMALL TAPS FROM GUDGEON HAVE RESULTED. I'M BEGINNING TO FEED SMALL AMOUNTS OF HEMP AND CASTERS AT POINTS A AND B. I'LL FISH THE MIDDLE ON THE WAGGLER AND POINT B ON THE 10 METRE POLE.

A CLASSIC CAPELS ROACH, A MINT CONDITIONED 14oz FISH. IT GAVE A GOOD ACCOUNT OF ITSELF ON LIGHT GEAR TOO, BUT THE ELASTIC REDRESSED THE SITUATION. EVEN WITH SUCH A FINE LINE YOU DON'T FEEL WORRIED IF YOU CAN GET THE ELASTIC/LINE RATIO RIGHT.

THAT'S FUNNY. BITES HAVE CEASED. IT'S PROBABLY BECAUSE THE EARLY MIST IS CLEARING AND THE SUN'S PUSHING THROUGH.

PERHAPS THE FISH HAVE MOVED OUT. I'LL GIVE THE WAGGLER A TRY.

A CAREFUL APPROACH IS NEEDED HERE ALSO. I'VE SET THE RIG A GOOD 18in OVER-DEPTH — THIS MEANS OVER-CASTING AND RETRIEVING THE END TACKLE TO GET IT WORKING CORRECTLY.

Grand Union Canal Continued

● If you like the look of Lady Capels, check before fishing that day tickets are still obtainable on the bank. Litter problems along this stretch became so bad that the controlling club issued a warning that day permits would be withdrawn unless there was an improvement. They were forced to act because the litter louts had jeopardised their long term control of the fishings.

WELL IT'S NO GOOD SITTING HERE NOT GETTING BITES. I'M GOING TO SCALE DOWN ON THE WAGGLER. I'VE BEEN FISHING A 1lb BOTTOM AND 18 FINE WIRE HOOK WITH MICRO SHOT DOWN THE RIG. LET'S TRY 12oz AND A 20 HOOK WITH 3 TINY STYL WEIGHTS SPREAD OUT.

1.5 lb.
Styl
Styl
Styl
12oz
Size 20 Fine Wire

I'VE GOT ONE GOOD ROACH IN THE NET AND BUMPED ANOTHER, BUT IT'S A REAL STRUGGLE IN THE BRIGHT SUN, WITH THE CANAL AS CLEAR AS TAP WATER.

ONE TRICK THAT OFTEN GETS YOU A BITE ON THESE TYPE OF DAYS IS TO KEEP TWITCHING YOUR FLOAT IN A FEW INCHES. THIS MOVES THE HOOKBAIT ALONG THE BOTTOM . . . .

. . . AND A FISH THAT'S BEEN A BIT UNSURE WILL OFTEN GRAB THE BAIT BY INSTINCT LIKE THIS ONE DID!

THREE GOOD ROACH, NOW I'VE HOOKED SOMETHING BIGGER. THIS ONE TOOK ON—THE-DROP.

I'VE REALLY GOT 'EM GOING NOW! WONDER WHAT THIS IS? IT IS'NT A CHUB, THE FIGHT IS TOO PONDEROUS.

A 1½ lb BREAM. THIS IS TURNING INTO A NICE MIXED CATCH.

I TOOK ANOTHER BREAM ON THE WAGGLER AND THOUGHT I'D HAVE ONE MORE CHUCK IN ON THE POLE BEFORE I GO. I'M STRAIGHT INTO A BIG FISH.

DECEMBER
Hampshire Avon
near Christchurch

THE SPOT I'VE CHOSEN HAS BEEN DICTATED BY THE ALMOST IMPOSSIBLE CONDITIONS. IT'S NOT THE MOST OBVIOUS SWIM FOR THE EXPECTED SPECIES HERE, CHUB AND BARBEL.

WIND AND RAIN

EDDY

5ft

6ft

4ft

SHALLOWS

GRAVEL RUN

BUT I'VE FOUND A SMALL GRAVEL RUN THIS SIDE OF THE MIDDLE. MY FINE APPROACH AND REGULAR LOOSE FEEDING METHODS SHOULD EVENTUALLY DRAW SOME FISH IN.

SHALLOWS

FRED'S USING HIS TRUSTED SPLIT-CANE ROD AND CENTREPIN REEL. IT'S INTERESTING THAT HE DOESN'T PUT LASHINGS OF FEED DOWN AND ALSO TENDS TO SELECT SWIMS MANY ANGLERS WOULD IGNORE.

FRED'S METHODS

FRED HAS CAUGHT 170 BARBEL THIS SEASON. HIS BIGGEST CAME FROM THIS VENUE AND WEIGHED OVER 9lb. RIGS 1-3 ARE USED IN HIS MAIN SWIM. RIG 4 IS FOR ROVING AND SEARCHING OUT ODD BIG BARBEL.

— John Wilson

NEARLY 4lb, THAT FISH. A NICE START! IT GAVE A VERY FINICKY BITE THOUGH, EVEN ON A 1·7lb HOOKLENGTH AND 18 HOOK. I'LL KEEP REGULAR HELPINGS OF HEMP AND CASTER GOING IN AND TRY SINGLE CASTER ON THE HOOK.

I'M EXPERIMENTING WITH A NEW RIG. MY BULK SHOT IS A LONG STRING OF Nº 8s. MICHEL CUREAU, THE FRENCH INTERNATIONAL, SHOTS ALL HIS POLE RIGS IN SIMILAR FASHION. THOUGHT I'D TRY A HEAVIER VERSION ON RUNNING LINE.

SMALL ALL BALSA FLOAT

2·6lb

Nº 8s

1·7lb

Nº 8

Nº 10

18 BARBLESS

SMALLER SHOTS WITH SMALL GAPS BETWEEN OFFER LESS RESISTANCE AGAINST THE FLOW THAN LARGER ONES.

Nº 8s

Nº 4s

Hampshire Avon Continued

● Fred Crouch is a rare breed of angler — he has concentrated exclusively on barbel for more than 30 years. He is famous for crossing swords with those who claim barbel in the late teens of pounds are there for the taking. According to Fred, giant barbel are very thin on the ground — and many of the monster sightings are mythical.

A BIT OVER 3lb, THIS ONE I'D SAY.

I'VE JUST HOOKED MY SECOND AVON FISH OF THE SESSION — ANOTHER NICE CHUB. THE WIND'S SO VICIOUS NOW I'M HAVING TO HOLD ON TO MY BROLLY AT TIMES.

I HAD SMALL TWITCHES ON THE QUIVERTIP IMMEDIATELY I CHANGED OVER TO THE BOMB. THE BITES AREN'T DEVELOPING THOUGH — MISSED THAT ONE.

I DON'T THINK THE TWITCH BITES ARE SMALL FISH — I'D HAVE HOOKED ONE BY NOW.

I'VE HAD THIS FISH ON FOR 10 MINUTES NOW, AND I'VE HAD TO LEAVE THE COMFORT OF MY BROLLY, AS IT GOT SIDEWAYS ON IN THE CURRENT AND THREATENED TO MOVE INTO THE SHALLOWS ROUND TO MY LEFT. IT'S OBVIOUSLY A NICE BARBEL.

BY NOT USING TOO POWERFUL A ROD I'VE MANAGED TO TURN THE FISH INTO THE SHALLOWS. IT'S AMAZING THE PRESSURE YOU CAN APPLY TO LIGHT LINES IF THE ROD MATCHES — NEARLY THERE.

FRED CROUCH IS STILL TUCKED AWAY UNDER HIS BROLLY TOO. SO FAR HE'S ONLY HAD ONE MISSED BITE.

MY SWIM HAS GONE DEAD ON THE FLOAT. LET'S TRY PUTTING A FEW FEEDER LOADS OF HEMP AND CASTERS OUT. I'VE BEEN LOOSEFEEDING BUT I'M NOT SURE HOW MUCH IS STAYING IN THE SWIM.

FLOW

LOOSE FEED HAS BEEN GOING IN HERE.

LANDING ON BOTTOM HERE

I'VE DEPOSITED SEVERAL FEEDER LOADS AT POINT B. NOW I THINK I'LL SWITCH TO A BOMB LINK. IT'S A BIT LOW AND CLEAR TO KEEP CRASHING OUT THE FEEDER.

B

FEED TRUNDLING ALONG BOTTOM

SHALLOWS

4·4-lb BAYER

TWISTED NYLON LINK

KNOT

LOOP ATTACHMENT

LINK SWIVEL

2·6-lb BAYER

18 DRENNAN SPECIALIST

¼ oz BOMB

A REALLY POSITIVE TAKE AT LAST — THE QUIVERTIP PULLED FORWARDS AND DROPPED BACK VIOLENTLY. THOSE SMALLER INDICATIONS MUST HAVE BEEN LINERS FROM A BIG FISH. THIS IS REALLY POWERFUL.

RATHER THAN USE THE NET, I'VE GENTLY STEERED THE BARBEL ON TO THIS SANDY BEACH.

NOT BAD, THREE FISH FOR 14-lb ON A DAY WHEN MOST METHODS WOULD BE DOOMED TO FAILURE. THE BARBEL WEIGHED 6lb 14oz, RATHER A LEAN FISH — IT LOOKED NEARER 8lb. THE CHUB WENT 3lb 12oz AND 3lb 6oz. POOR FRED'S JINX CONTINUES, HE DIDN'T GET ANY ACTION. STILL HE'S NOT WORRIED, HE'LL SOON BE AMONGST THE FISH AGAIN. MY LIGHTER MATCH APPROACH MADE ALL THE DIFFERENCE TODAY. I MUST SAY WHEN YOU DO GET A FISH ON THE AVON IT'S A BIG 'UN. THERE DON'T SEEM TO BE ANY SMALL FISH ABOUT — OR IF THERE ARE THEY MUST BE VERY LOCALISED. STRANGE, BECAUSE THE TYPE OF SWIM I FISHED WOULD NORMALLY HOLD PLENTY OF SMALL STUFF.

DECEMBER
Nottingham Embankment
River Trent, Nottinghamshire

FISHING IS FREE FROM THE EMBANKMENT STEPS AND IT'S PERFECT STICK WATER. I'VE SET UP A LIGNUM STICK RIG, USING PAIRS OF Nº 8s FOR MY MAIN WEIGHTING. I CAN'T GET ON WITH BIGGER NON-TOXIC SHOT FOR THIS JOB. I'M EXPERIMENTING WITH A COUPLE OF STYL WEIGHTS AS DROPPERS.

Lignum stickfloat
Nº 8s
Nº 8s
Nº 8s
Nº 8s
1·5 lb
Nº 6s
Nº 10 styl
1 lb
Nº 10 styl

I'VE DRIVEN UP THE M1 IN THICK FOG FOR A DAYS FISHING WITH FELLOW MAIL COLUMNIST FRANK BARLOW. IT PROMISES TO BE A RIGHT LAUGH. FRANK'S GOT A TREMENDOUS SENSE OF HUMOUR, BUT HE'S EQUALLY FAMOUS IN THE MIDLANDS FOR HIS ABILITY WITH THE STICKFLOAT. WE'RE ON FRANK'S HOME TRENT WATERS AT NOTTINGHAM EMBANKMENT. HE LIVES JUST ACROSS THE RIVER WITH HIS LOVELY WIFE MO AND THREE SONS.

HE TELLS ME IT'S SOLID WITH FISH, BUT THERE'S JUST ONE SMALL SNAG — WE'VE PICKED A MONDAY. APPARENTLY THE TRENT ALWAYS SWITCHES OFF ON THIS DAY BECAUSE OF THE WAY THE POWER STATIONS OPERATE.
IS HE WINDING ME UP?

... A NICE ROACH OF ABOUT 14oz. FRANK'S BEEN JOINED BY HIS MATE BUTANE WHO HE SUSPECTS IS TRYING TO MUSCLE HIS WAY INTO THE DIARY. THE LEG-PULLING IS NOW IN FULL FLOW BUT I'M AFRAID WE CAN'T SAY THE SAME OF THE FISHING —
BITES ARE VERY SPASMODIC.

A COUPLE OF SMALL ROACH FOLLOW AND NOW HE'S HIT INTO SOMETHING BETTER....

MEANWHILE FRANK'S HOOKED A CHUB WHICH IS SOMETHING OF A RARITY FOR THESE PEGS.

I TOOK A COUPLE OF NICE ROACH AND BUMPED OUT OF A CHUB, BUT SPORT SUDDENLY DIED AWAY. FRANK SWITCHED TO THE WAGGLER, BUT APART FROM A FEW MORE ROACH HIS SWIM HAS DIED TOO. IT SEEMS THE RIVER NEEDS AN INFLUX OF RAIN WATER TO GET IT OUT OF THE DOLDRUMS.

INDEX